ANNE MORROW LINDBERGH
THE LITERARY REPUTATION

GARLAND REFERENCE LIBRARY
OF THE HUMANITIES
(VOL. 556)

ANNE MORROW LINDBERGH
THE LITERARY REPUTATION

A Primary and Annotated Secondary Bibliography

Trude Wurz

GARLAND PUBLSHING, INC. • NEW YORK & LONDON
1988

Library of Congress Cataloging-in-Publication Data

Wurz, Trude, 1926–
    Anne Morrow Lindbergh: the literary reputation: a primary and
annotated secondary bibliography / Trude Wurz.
        p.   cm.—(Garland reference library of the humanities;
    v. 556)
    Includes index.
    ISBN 0–8240–7248–0 (alk. paper)
    1. Lindbergh, Anne Morrow, 1906–   —Bibliography.   I. Title.
II. Series: Garland reference library of the humanities; vol. 556.
Z8505.55.W87   1988
[PS3523.I516]
016.818'5209—dc19   88–12064
                                                                    CIP

Permission to reprint excerpts, titles, copyrights for *A Gift from the Sea*
and *The Unicorn and Other Poems, 1935–1955* granted by Anne
Morrow Lindbergh and Pantheon Books, a Division of Random
House, Inc. Permission to reprint descriptive entries from *North to the
Orient, Listen! The Wind, The Wave of the Future, The Steep Ascent,
Dearly Beloved, Earth Shine, Bring Me a Unicorn, Hour of Gold, Hour
of Lead, Locked Rooms and Open Doors, The Flower and the Nettle,*
and *The Journey Not the Arrival* granted by Harcourt Brace
Jovanovich, Inc. Permission to include extracts from *Bring Me a
Unicorn* granted by Anne Morrow Lindbergh and Chatto & Windus.

Printed on acid-free, 250-year-life paper
Manufactured in the United States of America

For
Mother and Father
And
Robert Hooper Wurz
R. Tim Wurz, James B. Wurz

FROM ALPHA TO OMEGA

CONTENTS

ACKNOWLEDGMENTS

For her gracious response to a variety of requests and
helpful guidance, and for her consent to publish this bibliography
I express my deep gratitude and appreciation to Mrs. Anne
(Spencer) Morrow Lindbergh.

My great indebtedness is to Dr. Roger R. Easson, Professor
of English at Memphis State University whose assistance was
vital to the preparation of this book. To him is due all credit
for his direct contributions. I emphasize my great appreciation
and gratitude for his interest, support, and invaluable
suggestions.

I am obligated to the editors of Garland Publishing, Inc.,
for their tireless patience and rare ability to understand
delays. I thank Mary Grace Smith, my first contact, and Paula
Landenburg, my recent advisor at Garland. Others, especially
Pam Chergotis, Linda Henry, Larry Davidow, Julia Johnson, Marie
Ellen Larcada, Phyllis Korper, Richard Koreto, all deserve my
sincere gratitude.

This book could not have been published without the assistance
of Camilla Shestopal at Chatto & Windus . Ltd. and The Hogarth
Press, Ltd., and Harcourt Brace Jovanovich, Inc. staff members,
Betty Schlossberg, Kathryn Naughton, Cynthia A. Bailie, Ginger

Boyer, Linda Holmes, Marisa, Miriam Phelps, and Warren Wallenstein.
To all of them and to Grace W. Budd, my warm gratitude. To
Pantheon Books, A Division of Random House, Inc., Ann Sandhorst,
Susan Di Sesa, Helena Franklin, Linda Smith, Gerald Summer,
and Linda Tennell I acknowledge my deep gratitude. I thank
Rosemary M. Peppet, Anne V. Waldburger, Judith Schiff; G.K. Hall
and Co., Jill O'Connell, Leslie Sanders; Louis A. Weil, Jr.;
former President Gerald R. Ford; Senator Jim Sasser of Tennessee,
Joni McFarland, Claire Peterson; Michael Burton who assisted
me with volutes difficulties; Noel Polk at the University of
Southern Mississippi; Miriam E. Phelps of Publishers Weekly
Library; Congressional Liaison Officer Channing E. Phillips;
Diane Lay of United States National Bureau of Standards; Cheryl
Hyer, David Hughett, Catherine Procter and Martha Young at
Vanderbilt University; Sue Craft Turpin, Rhodes College; David
Sparks, and Marcie Rarick at Notre Dame University; Guy Thomas
Mendina, Dr. John L. Dameron, Dr. Joseph K. Davis, Dr. Kay P.
Easson, Dr. Henry H. Peyton, Linda Dinwiddie, Joy Bailey Dunn,
Earline W. Gabriel, Deborah Brackstone, Paula Barnett, Martha
Earheart, Mary Sinclair, Stan Whitehorn and Marrin T. Fleet at
Memphis State University; University of Mississippi librarians
Zabi Rezaee and Zacharia Thomas; Memphis/Shelby Public Library,
Douglas Marsh, Frank Beardsley, Jan Shaw, Carol Smith, Debbie
Gray, Jeff Thomas, Bobby Flanary, Francis French, Denise Sphinx,
Irma H. Roberts, George W. Holmes; Pete and Frank Canon of
Central Printing Co.; Eddie Clinton of Clinton Graphics, Inc.;

Murray Koodish of The Commercial Appeal; Process One Pictures;

Burke's Book Store; Cursey Roberson; AT & T Supervisor M. Hendren;

Mamie Lopez; Eileen Lawrence, Violet Schichtel, R. Tim Wurz,

James B. Wurz, and many others to whom I thank for their

assistance. Finally, I should like to thank my patient, supportive,

husband, Robert Hooper Wurz, who responded graciously at all

times with gentleness and contributions too numerous to mention.

T.K. Wurz

Since no other comprehensive Anne Morrow Lindbergh
bibliography, annotated or otherwise, has been compiled, with
a leap of faith, I undertake this project remembering Aristotle's
profound statement in Book I On Happiness, "Every art or applied
science and every systematic investigation, and similarly every
action and choice, seem to aim at some good."

I have been guided by various considerations. Obstacles
involved in collecting first editions, sui generis, and foreign
translations are so formidable as to be impossible to research
or collect.

Guides such as How to Identify and Collect American First
Editions, A Guide Second Edition, Revised, Jack Tannen, Arco
Publishing, Inc., New York, 1976, 1985 and First Editions: A
Guide to Identification Statements of Selected North American,

<u>British Commonwealth</u>, <u>and Irish Publishers on Their Methods</u>
<u>of Designating First Editions</u>, edited by Edward Zempel and Linda
A. Verkler, The Spoon River Press, 1984, however, were consulted.

From the wealth of materials I have selected those features
that seem to have the greatest merit. Awards, Honors, Interviews,
Letters, Radio Addresses, Filmstrips are listed under <u>Miscellanea</u>.
All major indices have been consulted and a checklist is included.

Writings of A.M. Lindbergh are to be found in section <u>A</u>
Books, <u>B</u> Articles, Essays, Preface, <u>C</u> Poems; writings about A.M.
Lindbergh in section D. The last section contains the Index.
Some Big Print, Books for Blind, and some foreign publishers
of Mrs. Lindbergh's works, and some excerpts are noted
simultaneously with the books reproduced in definitive form.
The time period covers the years 1928 to 1978.

The finished product is a representative rather than an
exhaustive record. Limitation of what could be included is
necessary so that research can continue. The aim of this bibliography is to assemble a convenient and useful record of books,
articles, essays, and poems written by AML and about AML primarily
because of the historical value of aviation. No bibliography, however, serves fully the needs in which it might be employed. This
book is presented as a rough sketch of the times and conditions
during the years 1928 to 1978.

The author does not represent that these pages are an all-inclusive list of writings by and about Anne Lindbergh. This book does contain material that has been found after diligent and exhaustive search spanning fifty years.

Mechanics

"Collation" is not meant to compare texts or statements in order to note points of agreement or disagreement. The word is used for verification of the number, and order of the leaves, and signatures of a volume. All signatures leaves are stitched. No paperback books are described.

Titles of poems and articles are enclosed in quotation marks. The book title-pages are transcribed in full by the method called quasi-facsimile, recording all letters and symbols printed on the pages.

Index items are referred to by the various sections in alphabetical and numeral order, and not by page number of book.

Brackets are placed for editorial interpolations.

Only two kinds of type are used, Roman and italic.

No distinction is made between bold and small capital letters in the books.

Chapter headings and numerals are separated before mention of text material is made.

Roman numerals are printed in front matter of book and Arabic numerals on text pages.

Vergules are used to separate each line during descriptions of
board covers, spine stampings, and during reproductions of title-
pages, half-title pages, and copyright pages.
Pages numbered but not printed in the section under "Pagination"
are enclosed in brackets.
Wove paper has sometimes been noted as "antique paper."
Rough edges are labelled deckle-edged.
Top edges of pages are referred to as "head"; bottom edges as
"foot"; side of pages as "fore-edges."
Cover front bindings are listed as "upper"; back covers as
"lower."
Location of photographs in the books are not included in page
count, but inserts of photographs are listed between the
previous and subsequent pages.
Items in the primary bibliography are listed chronologically
by year and alphabetically by book title within each year.
Annotated items in the secondary bibliography are listed
chronologically by year and alphabetically by author's name
within each year. Anonymous articles are listed alphabetically
by title at the beginning of each month, each year.
Items that have not been located are listed and marked "Not
Seen."

MISCELLANEA

<u>Awards</u>

1933 National Trophy, The International League of Aviators

1933 Cross of Honor, Flag Association

1934 Gold Medal for Meritorious Radio Service, Veterans

Wireless Operators Association

1934 Gold Medal, First Woman to Receive Hubbard Gold Medal,

National Geographic Society

1935 Honorary M.A. Degree, Smith College in Massachusetts

1939 Honorary LL.D. Degree, Amherst College, and University

of Rochester

1939 American Booksellers Association Award

1940 Charles Despiau Bronze Sculpture of Head of Anne Morrow

Lindbergh

1940 Charles Despiau Bronze Sculpture of Head of AML Presented

to Modern Museum

<u>Interviews</u>

Whitman, Alden. "A Conversation With Anne Morrow Lindbergh."

<u>Ladies</u> <u>Home</u> <u>Journal</u>, 93 (May 1976) 68, 70, 178, 180, 186.

Whitman, Alden. "Anne Morrow Lindbergh Reminisces About Life

With Lindy." The New York Times Biography Service,
(8 May 1977) 16-18, 22, 26, 28.
Sevareid, Arnold Eric. "A Conversation With Anne Morrow
Lindbergh." Encyclopedia Americana/CBS News Audio Resource
Library c #05773, (23 May 1977).
Thrush, Robin A. "A Hero's Wife Remembers, A Rare Interview."
Good Housekeeping, 184 (June 1977) 74, 76, 78, 80, 82.

Letters

"Letters to the Editor." The New York Times, 83 (16 Dec. 1933) 14.
Patterson, Jean Rushmore. "Letter to Anne Lindbergh." New
York: The Lenox Hill Press, 1940, p. 19.
Waters, Caroline S. "Letters to the Editor." The New York
Times Book Review, (17 Nov. 1940) 2.
Mallett, Bertha B. "Letters to the Editor." Christian Century,
57 (27 Nov. 1940) 1485.
"Speaking of 'Past Formulas' Letters to the Times." The
New York Times, 90 (13 Jan. 1941) 14.
Bush, Dorothy, Susan Comegys, Mavise Crocker, Betty DeWitt,
Jean Markle Haverford, Kathryn Hubbard, Elvadolis Johnson,
Dorothy Englehard Lane, Blanche Leonard, Christine Lillie, Sue
McCann, Lillian Miller, Gwendolyn Newton, Agnes Reid, Janet
Johnson Somers, Virginia Thorpe, Ann Waitz. "Dear Mrs.
Lindbergh." Life, 39 (3 Oct. 1955) 118-127.
Flanders, Ila M.K. "Letters to the Editor." Saturday Review,
23 (2 Feb. 1957) 23.

Kogan, Herman. "Letters to the Editor." <u>Saturday</u> <u>Review</u>, 23
(2 Feb. 1957) 23.

Nye, George P. "Letters to the Editor." <u>Saturday</u> <u>Review</u>, 23
(2 Feb. 1957) 23.

Clark, Laura W. "Letters to the Editor." <u>Saturday</u> <u>Review</u>, 23
(16 Feb. 1957) 23-4.

Clendon, Earl. "Letters to the Editor." <u>Saturday</u> <u>Review</u>, 23
(16 Feb. 1957) 23-4.

Cross, Rose. "Letters to the Editor." <u>Saturday</u> <u>Review</u>, 23
(16 Feb. 1957) 23-4.

Knevels, M.E. "Letters to the Editor." <u>Saturday</u> <u>Review</u>, 23
(16 Feb. 1957) 23-4.

Shea, Adellia P. "Letters to the Editor." <u>Saturday</u> <u>Review</u>,
23 (16 Feb. 1957) 23-4.

<u>Radio</u>

"The Wind of Privation Or the Sun of Mercy?" The National
Broadcasting System, Philadelphia, American Friends Service
Committee, (24 Dec. 1940).

"Anne Asks Food For Europeans." The National Broadcasting
System, (25 Dec. 1940).

<u>Filmstrips</u>

"An African Essay." /2 filmstrips (70 & 78 frs.) 35mm. 2 cassettes/
Guidance Associates. Pleasantville, N.Y., 1969.

Publications Indexed - Book Review Index 1978

Publications of the Modern Language Association of America

Reader's Guide to Periodical Literature

Reference Book Review Index

Small Press Record of Books in Print

Subject Guide to Children's Books in Print

The Times Index

Twentieth Century Authors: A Biographical Dictionary of

  Modern Literature

Wall Street Review of Books

Whitaker's Cumulative Book List

Who's Who in America: A Biographical Dictionary of Notable

  Living Men and Women

Who's Who: An Annual Biographical Dictionary

Who's Who of American Women

Women Studies Abstracts

World Literature Since 1945

Year's Work in English Studies

ABBREVIATIONS

AML   Anne Morrow Lindbergh

BMU   Bring Me A Unicorn
                Diaries and Letters of Anne Morrow Lindbergh
                1922 - 1928

DB   Dearly Beloved A Theme and Variations

ES   Earth Shine

FN   The Flower and the Nettle
                Diaries and Letters of Anne Morrow Lindbergh
                1936 - 1939

GS   Gift from the Sea

HGHL   Hour of Gold, Hour of Lead
                Diaries and Letters of Anne Morrow Lindbergh
                1929 - 1932

JNA   The Journey Not the Arrival

LW   Listen! the Wind

LROD   Locked Rooms and Open Doors
                Diaries and Letters of Anne Morrow Lindbergh
                1933 - 1935

NO   North to the Orient

SA   The Steep Ascent

UOP   The Unicorn and Other Poems

WF   The Wave of the Future
                A Confession of Faith

I.

WRITINGS BY A.M. LINDBERGH

WRITINGS BY A.M. LINDBERGH

A

BOOKS

A1   NORTH <u>to the</u> ORIENT   1935

Issued in hard cover one-piece red linen binding over boards and
spine. Upper board /design feature/ airplane stamped in imitation
gold foil; spine stamped in imitation gold foil /across/ NORTH :
<u>to the</u> ORIENT : /design feature/ : ANNE MORROW : LINDBERGH :
HARCOURT, BRACE : AND COMPANY

Notes: Cream colored wove paper; head pages stained yellow; head
and foot edges trimmed; fore-edges deckle-edged

Maps on lining papers, and on front <u>recto</u> and back <u>verso</u> end
pages

Between pages 2 and 3, one white glossy page uncounted; <u>recto</u>
blank; <u>verso</u> photo

COLLATION: 4° 16 signatures; stitched

PAGINATION: /1-4/ 5-13 /14/ 15-255 /256/

CONTENTS: End page; 1 part-title; 2 blank; 3 title-page NORTH :
<u>to the</u> ORIENT : BY ANNE MORROW LINDBERGH : WITH MAPS BY CHARLES A.
LINDBERGH : New York: Harcourt, Brace and Company; 4 COPYRIGHT,
1935, BY : ANNE MORROW LINDBERGH : <u>All rights reserved</u>. <u>No part</u>
<u>of this book may</u> : <u>be reproduced in any form without permis</u>- :
<u>sion in writing from the publishers</u>, except <u>by</u> : <u>a reviewer who</u>
<u>may quote not more than</u> 300 : <u>words or reproduce not more than</u>
<u>three maps</u> : <u>in a review to be printed in a magazine or</u> :
<u>newspaper</u>. : PRINTED IN THE UNITED STATES OF AMERICA : BY QUINN &

BODEN COMPANY, INC., RAHWAY, N.J. ⁞ <u>Typography</u> <u>by</u> <u>Robert</u> <u>Josephy</u>;
5-6 CONTENTS; 7-13 PREFACE; 14 blank; 15 map ⁞ I. NORTH TO THE
ORIENT ⁞ text; 16-22 text; 23 II. PREPARATION ⁞ text; 24-36 text;
37 map ⁞ III. TAKE-OFF ⁞ text; 38-45 text; 46 map ⁞ IV. NORTH HAVEN ⁞
text; 47-53 text; 54 map ⁞ V. RADIO AND ROUTES ⁞ text; 55-63 text;
64 map ⁞ VI. BAKER LAKE ⁞ text; 65-79 text; 80 map ⁞ VII. AKLAVIK ⁞
text; 81-94 text; 95 map ⁞ VIII. POINT BARROW ⁞ text; 96-110 text;
111 map ⁞ IX. DARK ⁞ text; 112-121 text; 122 /invitation/ ⁞ X.
THE KING ISLANDERS ⁞ text; 123-132 text; 133 map ⁞ XI. KAMCHATKA ⁞
text; 134-147 text; 148 map ⁞ XII. FOG ⁞ --AND THE CHISHIMA ⁞
text; 149-162 text; 163 map ⁞ XIII. THE SINGING SAILORS ⁞ text;
164-173 text; 174 map ⁞ XIV. A FISHERMAN'S HUT ⁞ text; 175-182
text; 183 map ⁞ XV. THE PAPER ⁞ AND STRING OF LIFE ⁞ text;
184-193 text; 194 map ⁞ XVI. STOWAWAY ⁞ text; 195-198 text; 199
map ⁞ XVII. A RIVER ⁞ text; 200-204 text; 205 map ⁞ XVIII. THE
WALL ⁞ OF NANKING ⁞ text; 206-209 text; 210 map ⁞ XIX. THE
FLOODS ⁞ text; 211-221 text; 222 XX. THE MOST ⁞ BEAUTIFUL PAGODA ⁞
text; 223-225 text; 226 map ⁞ XXI. INTO THE YANGTZE ⁞ text;
227-234 text; 235 map ⁞ XXII. "SAYONARA" ⁞ text; 236-239 text; 240
XXIII. FLYING AGAIN ⁞ text; 241-244 text; 245-255 APPENDIX /list of
EMERGENCY EQUIPMENT FOR FORCED LANDING ON LAND (ORIENT FLIGHT--1931);
EMERGENCY EQUIPMENT FOR FORCED LANDING AT SEA (ORIENT FLIGHT--1931);
EMERGENCY EQUIPMENT FOR PARACHUTE JUMP (ORIENT FLIGHT--1931);
EMERGENCY FOOD PROVISIONS (ORIENT FLIGHT--1931); PERSONAL FLYING
EQUIPMENT (ORIENT FLIGHT--1931); PERSONAL EQUIPMENT (ORIENT

FLIGHT--1931); RADIO EQUIPMENT (ORIENT FLIGHT--1931); NAVIGATION

EQUIPMENT (ORIENT FLIGHT--1931); PLANE AND ENGINE EQUIPMENT

(ORIENT FLIGHT--1931); LOG OF FLIGHT TO ORIENT--1931; History of

Sirius/ 256 blank; end page.

+   +   +   +   +

Supplementary notes:

Other publications of NORTH to the ORIENT of noteworthy mention

1. 1935 London, Chatto & Windus

2. Translations:

    1935 French-Paris, Flon

    1935 Swedish-Stockholm, P.A. Norstedt

    1937 German-Leipsig, E.F. Tal

    1939 Italian-Firenze, Marzocco

3. Excerpts:

    Reader's Digest 30 (April 1937): 105-121

    "Airplane." A collection of Travel in America By Various

        Hands. Edited by George Bradshaw. New York: Farrar,

        Straus and Company, 1948, pp. 194-198

    "Dark." Fireside Book of Flying Stories. Edited by

        Paul Jensen. New York: Simon and Schuster, 1951,

        pp. 247-252

A2   LISTEN! the WIND   1938

Issued in hard cover one-piece carmen color linen cloth over upper
and lower boards and spine. Outline of airplane stamped in
imitation gold foil on upper board; spine stamped in imitation
gold foil /across/ LISTEN! ┇ the ┇ WIND ┇ /design feature/ ┇ ANNE
MORROW ┇ LINDBERGH ┇ HARCOURT, BRACE ┇ AND COMPANY

Notes: Cream colored wove paper; all edges trimmed

Maps on lining papers, and on front recto and back verso end
pages

Between pages 264 and 265 recto, photo of THE TINGMISSARTOQ;
verso blank

COLLATION: 4° 18 signatures; stitched

PAGINATION: /i-iv/ v-ix /x/ xi-xii /1-2/ 3-118 /119-120/ 121-217
/218-220/ 221-264 /photo page/ 265-275 /276/

CONTENTS: End page; i half-title /design feature/; ii By the same
author ┇ NORTH TO THE ORIENT; iii title-page Listen! the Wind ┇
BY ANNE MORROW LINDBERGH ┇ WITH FOREWORD AND MAP DRAWINGS BY ┇
CHARLES A. LINDBERGH ┇ HARCOURT, BRACE AND COMPANY, NEW YORK; iv
COPYRIGHT, 1938, BY ┇ ANNE MORROW LINDBERGH ┇ All rights reserved.
No part of this book may ┇ be reproduced in any form without permis- ┇
sion in writing from the publishers except by ┇ a reviewer who may
quote not more than 300 ┇ words in a review to be printed in a
magazine ┇ or newspaper. ┇ Acknowledgment is made to the National
Geographic ┇ Magazine for permission to reprint certain paragraphs ┇

from "Flying Around the North Atlantic" by Anne ⁞ Morrow Lindbergh ⁞ PRINTED IN THE UNITED STATES OF AMERICA ⁞ <u>Typography by Robert Josephy</u>; v FOREWORD ⁞ BY CHARLES A. LINDBERGH; x blank; xi-xii CONTENTS; 1 PART 1 ⁞ SANTIAGO; 2 map; 3 CHAPTER I ⁞ TAIL WIND ⁞ text; 4-6 text; 7 CHAPTER II ⁞ COULD WE LAND? ⁞ text; 8-16 text; 17 CHAPTER III ⁞ A TRANSATLANTIC BASE ⁞ text; 18-27 text; 28 CHAPTER IV ⁞ "WE ARE LOOKING ⁞ FOR SOME SHACKLES" ⁞ text; 29-37 text; 38 CHAPTER V ⁞ WHERE WOULD WE SLEEP? ⁞ text; 39-46 text; 47 CHAPTER VI ⁞ "I AM HERE CHEF" ⁞ text; 48-54 text; 55 CHAPTER VII ⁞ THERE WERE OTHER ROOMS ⁞ text; 56-67 text; 68 CHAPTER VIII ⁞ THE MORNING AND PLANS ⁞ text; 69-74 text; 75 CHAPTER IX ⁞ "BRAZIL? HE TWIRLED A BUTTON" ⁞ text; 76-83 text; 84 CHAPTER X ⁞ BACK TO DAKAR? ⁞ text; 85-88 text; 89 CHAPTER XI ⁞ CONTACT ⁞ text; 90-95 text; 96 CHAPTER XII ⁞ YELLOW FEVER ⁞ text; 97-100 text; 101 CHAPTER XIII ⁞ THE EMPTY BOX ⁞ text; 102-108 text; 109 CHAPTER XIV ⁞ "PLEASED TO GRANT ... " ⁞ text; 110-115 text; 116 CHAPTER XV ⁞ THOSE TOWERS ON THE HILL ⁞ text; 117-118 text; 119 PART 2 ⁞ BATHHURST; 120 map; 121 CHAPTER XVI ⁞ AND THE BRITISH ⁞ text; 122-129 text; 130 CHAPTER XVII ⁞ PIECES OF A PUZZLE ⁞ text; 131-138 text; 139 CHAPTER XVIII ⁞ LINES OF DEFENSE ⁞ text; 140-149 text; 150 CHAPTER XIX ⁞ OUR EARLY MORNINGS ⁞ text; 151-156 text; 157 CHAPTER XX ⁞ "IF WE TAKE OFF AT DAYBREAK--" ⁞ text; 158-164 text; 165 CHAPTER XXI ⁞ "IF WE HAD A WIND--" ⁞ text; 166-170 text; 171 CHAPTER XXII ⁞ "THE SUN AND STARS ARE MINE" ⁞ text; 172-176 text; 177 CHAPTER XXIII ⁞ "WITH A MOON--" ⁞ text; 178-182 text; 183 CHAPTER XXIV ⁞ "IF WE TAKE OFF AT NIGHT--" ⁞ text; 184-189 text; 190 CHAPTER XXV ⁞ EARTH-BOUND ⁞

text; 191-194 text; 195 CHAPTER XXVI ┊ A FEW TRICKS ┊ text;
196-202 text; 203 CHAPTER XXVII ┊ "LISTEN! THE WIND IS RISING" ┊
text; 204-217 text; 218 blank; 219 PART 3 ┊ BOUND NATAL; 220 map;
221 CHAPTER XXVIII ┊ MY LITTLE ROOM ┊ text; 222-229 text; 230
CHAPTER XXIX ┊ THE NIGHT ┊ text; 231-238 text; 239 CHAPTER XXX ┊
A DISTANT LIGHTHOUSE ┊ text; 240-243 text; 244 CHAPTER XXXI ┊
THE DAY ┊ text; 245-249 text; 250 CHAPTER XXXII ┊ "ALL THE LAMPS
ARE LIT" ┊ text; 251-260 text; 261 CHAPTER XXXIII ┊ "AND SHUT OUR
MINDS ┊ TO THE SEA" ┊ text; 262 text; 263-264 APPENDIX ┊ Compiled
by C.A.L. ⎽/list of INSTRUMENTS; PLANE'S RADIO EQUIPMENT⎽/; ⎽/recto
photo Museum and TINGMISSARTOQ; verso blank⎽/; 265-275 APPENDIX
⎽/list of PLANE'S RADIO EQUIPMENT; EMERGENCY RADIO EQUIPMENT;
AIRPLANE AND ENGINE EQUIPMENT; NAVIGATION EQUIPMENT; PERSONAL
FLYING EQUIPMENT; PERSONAL EQUIPMENT; PARACHUTE EQUIPMENT;
PHOTOGRAPHIC EQUIPMENT; EMERGENCY EQUIPMENT FOR FORCED LANDING ON
LAND; EMERGENCY EQUIPMENT FOR FORCED LANDING AT SEA; EMERGENCY
PROVISIONS; LOG OF ATLANTIC SURVEY FLIGHT: 1933⎽/; 276 blank;
end page.

+   +   +   +   +

Supplementary notes:

Other publications of LISTEN! the WIND of noteworthy mention

    1. n.d. Toronto, Mcclelland

    2. Translations:

        1938 Italian-Harper

1939 French-Paris, Corrès

1940 Hungarian-Budapest, Revai

1940 Italian-Milano, V. Bompiani

1956 Italian-Milano, A. Mondedor

1956 German-München, R. Piper

1973 French-Buchet/Chastel

n.d. German-Zurich, Orell Füsseli

3. Excerpts:

Reader's Digest 34 (April 1939): 111-128

THE GREAT EXPLORERS. Edited by Helen Wright and Samuel

    Rapport. New York: Harper & Brothers, Publishers,

    1957, pp. 594-615

A3   The Wave of the Future   1940
                           A CONFESSION OF FAITH

Issued in hard cover, one-piece black linen cloth over upper and

lower stiff boards and flat spine. Upper cover stamped in imitation

gold foil The Wave of the Future ⦂ A CONFESSION OF FAITH; spine

stamped in imitation gold foil ⎣down⎦ The Wave of the Future Anne

Morrow Lindbergh

Notes: Cream colored wove paper; heavy end pages front and back;

all edges trimmed

COLLATION: 4° 3 signatures; stitched

PAGINATION: /i-vi/ /1-2/ 3-41 /42/

CONTENTS: i-ii blank; iii half-title; iv by the same author; v
title-page The Wave of the Future ⋮ A CONFESSION OF FAITH ⋮ Anne
Morrow Lindbergh ⋮ /publisher's hb initials 2.02 cm. tied cursive/ ⋮
HARCOURT, BRACE AND COMPANY, NEW YORK; vi COPYRIGHT, 1940, BY ⋮ ANNE
MORROW LINDBERGH ⋮ All rights reserved, including ⋮ the right to
reproduce this book ⋮ or portions thereof in any form. ⋮ first
edition ⋮ PRINTED IN THE UNITED STATES OF AMERICA ⋮ BY QUINN &
BODEN COMPANY, INC., RAHWAY, N.J.; 1 /second/ half-title; 2 blank;
3-41 text; 42 blank.

        +   +   +   +   +

Supplementary note:

Other publication of The Wave of the Future A CONFESSION OF FAITH
of noteworthy mention

    Reader's Digest Condensed Books 37 (November 1940): 1-12

A4   THE STEEP ASCENT   1944

Issued in hard cover one-piece black filled-buckram over upper and
lower boards and spine. Spine stamped in white ink /down/ ANNE
MORROW LINDBERGH The Steep Ascent HARCOURT, BRACE ⋮ AND COMPANY

Notes: Cream colored wove paper; head pages stained in blue; head
and foot edges trimmed; fore-edges deckle-edged

COLLATION: 4° 8; 2° 1 signatures; stitched

PAGINATION: /2 pages uncounted fly-leaves7 /i-iv7 v-viii /ix-xii7

/1-27 3-120 /121-1227 /2 pages uncounted fly-leaves7

CONTENTS: i half-title; ii By the same author; iii title-page THE :

STEEP ASCENT : By Anne Morrow Lindbergh : Harcourt, Brace and

Company, New York; iv COPYRIGHT, 1944, BY : ANNE MORROW LINDBERGH :

All rights reserved, including : the right to reproduce this book :

or portions thereof in any form. : first edition : /design feature7 :

A WARTIME BOOK : This complete edition is produced in full : compliance

with the government's regu- : lations for conserving paper and other :

essential materials. : PRINTED IN THE UNITED STATES OF AMERICA;

v-vii PREFACE; ix "The quotation of Arthur Koestler in the" :

/acknowledgment of sources7; x blank; xi CONTENTS; xii blank; 1

fly-title; 2 blank; 3 I : GOOD-BYE : text; 4-9 text; 10 II : DUST

OF CONFUSION : text; 11-18 text; 19 III : THE HOUND OF TIME : text;

20-25 text; 26 IV : TAKE OFF : text; 27-40 text; 41 V : ACHILLES,

O ACHILLES : text; 42-62 text; 63 VI : NO HAWK SO HIGH : text;

64-76 text; 77 VII : THE ANTEROOM : text; 78-101 text; 102 VIII :

LIKE A MAPLE SEED : text; 103-115 text; 116 IX : THIS THEN WAS

LIFE : text; 117-120 text; 121-122 blank.

+   +   +   +   +

Supplementary notes:

Other publications of THE STEEP ASCENT of noteworthy mention

   1. 1945 London, Chatto & Windus

      1955 Dell

2. Translation:

    1944 German-Tübingen, R. Wunderlich

3. Excerpt:

    The Treasure Chest An Anthology of Contemplative Prose.

    Edited by James Donald Adams. New York: E.P. DUTTON &

    COMPANY, INC., 1946, "The Living Dead" page 383; "The

    Inner Core" page 384

A5   GIFT FROM THE SEA   1955

Issued in three-piece flat back binding, stamped in four colors;

orange-brown color sea shells stamped on tan color upper and lower

paper boards; GIFT FROM THE SEA stamped in navy-blue ink on upper

board; spine navy-blue linen cloth with .07 cm. overlap on boards;

spine stamped in white ink /down/ GIFT FROM THE SEA ANNE MORROW

LINDBERGH PANTHEON

Notes: Cream colored laid paper; all edges trimmed

COLLATION: 4° 8 signatures; stitched

PAGINATION: /1-8/ 9-10 /11-14/ 15-16 /17-20/ 21-35 /36-38/ 39-58
/59-62/ 63-76 /77-78/ 79-87 /88-90/ 91-109 /110-112/ 113-120
/121-122/ 123-127 /128/

CONTENTS: End page; i /publisher's device/; 2 By the Same Author;

3 title-page Anne Morrow Lindbergh : GIFT FROM THE SEA : /shell

design/ : /swollen rule/ : /swollen rule/ : PANTHEON; 4 COPYRIGHT

1955 BY ANNE MORROW LINDBERGH : PUBLISHED BY PANTHEON BOOKS, INC. :

333 SIXTH AVENUE, NEW YORK 14, N.Y. : PUBLISHED SIMULTANEOUSLY IN

CANADA BY ⋮ MCCLELLAND & STEWART, LTD., TORONTO, CANADA ⋮ The
quotation on page 72 ⋮ is reprinted by courtesy ⋮ of Random House,
Inc. ⋮ LIBRARY OF CONGRESS CATALOG CARD NUMBER ⋮ 55-5065 ⋮
MANUFACTURED IN THE UNITED STATES OF AMERICA; 5 Contents; 6 blank;
7 half-title page; 8 blank; 9-11 /author's Foreword/ I began these
pages for myself, in order to think; 12 blank; 13 fly-title I ⋮
THE BEACH ⋮ /shell design/; 14 blank; 15-17 text; 18 blank; 19
fly-title II ⋮ CHANNELLED WHELK ⋮ /shell design/; 20 blank; 21-35
text; 36 blank; 37 fly-title III ⋮ MOON SHELL ⋮ /shell design/;
38 blank; 39-59 text; 60 blank; 61 fly-title IV ⋮ DOUBLE-SUNRISE ⋮
/shell design/ ⋮ 62 blank; 63-76 text; 77 fly-title V ⋮ OYSTER
BED ⋮ /shell design/; 78 blank; 79-88 text; 89 fly-title VI ⋮
ARGONAUTA ⋮ /shell design/; 90 blank; 91-110 text; 111 fly-title
VII ⋮ A FEW SHELLS ⋮ /shell design/; 112 blank; 113-120 text; 121
fly-title VIII ⋮ THE BEACH AT MY BACK ⋮ /shell design/; 122 blank;
123-128 text; end page.

+   +   +   +   +

Supplementary notes:
Other publications of GIFT FROM THE SEA of noteworthy mention
  1. 1955 F. Watts, A Keith Jennison Book; Large Print Edition
      1955 New American Library
      1965 American Printing House for the Blind, Louisville,
           Kentucky, Random House: Braille Edition
      1975 Pantheon Books, 20th Anniversary Edition

2. Translations:

   1955 German-München, R. Piper

   1956 Finnish-Helsinski, Söderström

   1956 Italian-Milano, V. Bompiani

   1956 Swedish-Stockholm, Norstedt

   1959 French-Paris, Livre Contemporain

3. Excerpts:

   Reader's Digest 66 (May 1955): 167-180, 182, 184, 186, 188

   "What I Learned from the Sea": National Wildlife 9 (December,
      1970-January 1971): 24-25

   McCall Magazine 102 (August 1975): 75-76, 106-112

4. Sound Recording:

   1955 Aetna Audio-Book Production Unit for the Connecticut
      State Library, Library for the Blind and Physically
      Handicapped, 2 cassettes; 15/16 ips. 2-track mono.

A6   THE UNICORN   1956
                        AND OTHER POEMS
                          1935-1955

Issued in three-piece flat back binding, stamped in two colors;
mulberry-red color feature design stamped on upper board; spine
tan color linen cloth with .07 cm. overlap on confederate-blue
upper and lower paper boards; spine stamped in navy-blue ink /down/
THE UNICORN ANNE MORROW LINDBERGH PANTHEON

Notes: Cream colored wove paper; all edges trimmed

COLLATION: 4° 6 signatures; stitched

PAGINATION: /i-iv7 /1-47 5-6 /7-87 9-18 /19-207 21-32 /33-347 35-47
/48-507 51-57 /58-607 61-73 /74-767 77-86 /87-927

CONTENTS: End page; i-iv blank; 1 /publisher's device7; 2 By the
Same Author; 3 title-page Anne Morrow Lindbergh : THE UNICORN :
AND OTHER POEMS : 1935-1955 : /swollen rule7; 4 COPYRIGHT Ⓒ 1956 BY
ANNE MORROW LINDBERGH : PUBLISHED BY PANTHEON BOOKS INC. : 333
SIXTH AVENUE, NEW YORK 14, N.Y. : PUBLISHED SIMULTANEOUSLY IN
CANADA BY : MCCLELLAND & STEWART, LTD., TORONTO, CANADA :
ACKNOWLEDGMENTS: : THE ATLANTIC MONTHLY, THE SATURDAY REVIEW : FIRST
EDITION, SEPTEMBER 1956 : SECOND PRINTING, SEPTEMBER 1956 : THIRD
PRINTING, SEPTEMBER 1956 : LIBRARY OF CONGRESS CATALOG CARD NUMBER: :
56-9810 : MANUFACTURED IN THE UNITED STATES OF AMERICA; 5-6 CONTENTS;
7 fly-title LOVE; 8 blank; 9 poem The Man and the Child; 10 poem
Alms; 11-12 poem The Little Mermaid; 13-14 poem Even--; 15 poem
Two Citadels; 16-17 poem A Leaf, a Flower, and a Stone; 18 poem
Interior Tree; 19 fly-title DEATH; 20 blank; 21-22 poem A Final Cry;
23-24 poem No Angels; 25 poem Elegy Under the Stars; 26 poem
Testament; 27 poem Presence; 28-29 poem Mountain; 30-31 poem All
Saints' Day; 32 poem Second Sowing; 33 fly-title CAPTIVE SPIRIT;
34 blank; 35 poem "Closing In"; 36-37 poem Security; 38-39 poem
Dogwood; 40-41 poem No Harvest Ripening; 42-43 poem The Stone; 44
poem Pilgrim; 45-47 poem Saint for Our Time; 48 blank; 49 fly-title
THE UNICORN; 50 blank; 51-57 poem The Unicorn in Captivity; 58
blank; 59 fly-title OPEN SKY; 60 blank; 61 poem Space; 62-64 poem
Winter Tree; 65 poem Pas de deux--Winter; 66-69 poem Ascent;
70-71 poem Flight of Birds; 72-73 poem Back to the Islands;

74 blank; 75 fly-title WIND OF TIME; 76 blank; 77 poem <u>Presentiment</u>;
78 poem <u>Within the Wave</u>; 79-81 poem <u>Family Album</u>; 82 poem <u>Broken
Shell</u>; 83-85 poem <u>Revisitation</u>; 86 poem <u>Bare Tree</u>; 87-92 blank;
end page.

+   +   +   +   +

Supplementary note:
Other publication of THE UNICORN AND OTHER POEMS 1935-1955 of
noteworthy mention
    1958 London, Chatto & Windus

A7   DEARLY BELOVED   1962
                        A <u>Theme</u> <u>and</u> <u>Variations</u>

Issued in hard cover three-piece white calico cloth over upper and
lower boards; confederate blue linen cloth over spine with 1.04 cm.
overlap on upper and lower boards; spine stamped in white foil
/down/ Anne Morrow Lindbergh _/design feature_/ _/#169 Baskerville
English mono_/ DEARLY BELOVED _/across_/ Harcourt, : Brace & : World
Notes: Cream colored wove paper; tweed weave blue lining on boards;
head and foot edges trimmed; fore-edges deckle-edged

COLLATION: 4° 13 signatures; stitched

PAGINATION: _/i-vi_/ _/1_/ 2-10 _/11_/ 12-16 _/17_/ 18-21 _/22-23_/ 24-41
_/42-43_/ 44-60 _/61_/ 62-73 _/74-75_/ 76-88 _/89_/ 90-102 _/103_/ 104-119
_/120-121_/ 122-133 _/134-135_/ 136-156 _/157_/ 158-174 _/175_/ 176-178
_/179_/ 180-188 _/189_/ 190-197 _/198-199_/ 200-202

CONTENTS: Multiple tropical blue heavy end page; i half-title; ii

By the same author /printed at foot of page/; iii title-page ANNE

MORROW LINDBERGH : DEARLY BELOVED : A Theme and Variations : /design

feature/ : A HELEN AND KURT WOLFF BOOK : HARCOURT, BRACE & WORLD,

INC., NEW YORK; iv copyright page Grateful acknowledgment is made

to Mrs. Norma Millay : Ellis for permisson /sic/ to quote from Edna

St. Vincent Millay's : "Prayer to Persephone," published by Harper

and Broth- : ers, copyright 1921, 1949, by Edna St. Vincent

Millay. : The excerpt from "Love and Marriage," music by James :

Van Heusen, words by Sammy Cahn, copyright 1955 by : Maraville Music

Corp., is used with permission. : /publisher's device/ : θ 1962 by

Harcourt, Brace & World, Inc. : Copyright in Canada 1962 by Harcourt,

Brace & World, Inc. : All rights reserved. No part of this book :

may be reproduced in any form or by any mechanical means, including

mimeograph : and tape recorder, without permission in writing from

the publisher. : First edition : Library of Congress Catalog Card

Number: 62-13520 : Printed in the United States of America;

v CONTENTS; vi blank; 1 fly-title Before : /design feature/; 2-10

text; 11 fly-title In This Company : /design feature/; 12-16 text;

17 fly-title The Wedding March : /design feature/; 18-21 text; 22

blank; 23 fly-title Deborah : /design feature/; 24-41 text; 42

blank; 43 fly-title Don : /design feature/; 44-60 text; 61 fly-title

Aunt Harriet : /design feature/; 62-73 text; 74 blank; 75 fly-title

Chrissie : /design feature/; 76-88 text; 89 fly-title André :

/design feature/; 90-102 text; 103 fly-title Beatrice : /design feature_/; 104-119 text; 120 blank; 121 fly-title Pierre ⋮ /design

feature_/; 122-133 text; 134 blank; 135 fly-title Frances ⋮

/design feature_/; 136-156 text; 157 fly-title Theodore ⋮ /design

feature_/; 158-174 text; 175 fly-title The Bride and Groom ⋮

/design feature_/; 176-178 text; 179 fly-title The Supper ⋮

/design feature_/; 180-188 text; 189 fly-title The Toast ⋮ /design

feature_/; 190-197 text; 198 blank; 199 fly-title After ⋮ /design

feature_/; 200-202 text; multiple tropical blue heavy end page.

+   +   +   +   +

Supplementary notes:

Other publications of DEARLY BELOVED A Theme and Variations of

noteworthy mention

   1. 1962 Toronto, Longmans

      McCall Magazine 89 (May 1962): 74-77, 154, 156, 158-160,

      162, 164, 166, 168

      Reader's Digest Condensed Books 4 (1962)

   2. Translations:

      1962 Danish-Købehavn, Thanning & Appels Forlag

      1964 German-Berlin, Deutsche Buch-Gemeinschaft

      1966 Spanish-Barcelona, Luis de Caralt

      1978 German-München, Deutschen Taschenbuch Verlag

A8   EARTH SHINE   1969

Issued in three-piece Italian blue linen cloth over upper and lower

boards; white linen cloth over flat spine with .05 cm. overlap on

boards; spine stamped in imitation gold foil /across/ rule :

/across/ rule : /across/ rule : /down/ EARTH SHINE : /across/

rule : /across/ rule : /across/ rule : /down/ Anne Morrow Lindbergh

Harcourt, Brace & World : /across/ /publisher's device/

Notes: White laid paper; confederate blue heavy paper lining on

boards; all edges trimmed. Plates, four leaves:

    Black-and white between 12-13, 28-29, 2nd and 3rd pages and

                    between 52-53, 60-61, 1st and 4th pages;

    Color   between 12-13, 28-29, 1st and 4th pages and

                    between 52-53, 60-61, 2nd and 3rd pages

COLLATION: 4° 6 signatures; stitched

PAGINATION: /i-vi/ vii-xiii /xiv-xviii/ /1-2/ 3-23 /24/ 25-29
/30/ 31-37 /38/ 39-45 /46-48/ 49-73 /74-76/

CONTENTS: End pages, one confederate blue heavy paper; one white

heavy paper; i half-title; ii blank; iii By the same author; iv

blank; v title-page Anne Morrow Lindbergh : EARTH SHINE : A Helen

and Kurt Wolff Book : Harcourt, Brace & World, Inc., New York :

/publisher's device/; vi copyright page Grateful acknowledgment is

made for the right to quote : From Last Poems of Elinor Wylie.

Copyright, 1943, by Alfred A. Knopf, : Inc. Reprinted by permission

of the publisher. : From "Little Gidding" in Four Quartets by

T.S. Eliot published by : Harcourt, Brace & World, Inc. and

reprinted with their permission. From "Time's Cap-Poem" in The Bright North by Abbie Huston Evans, published by The Macmillan Company. Reprinted by permis- sion of the author. Life Magazine originally published earlier versions of both essays. Copyright © 1966, 1969 by Anne Morrow Lindbergh All rights reserved. No part of this publication may be reproduced or transmitted in any form or by any means, electronic or mechanical, including photocopy, recording, or any information storage and retrieval system, without permission in writing from the publisher. First edition Library of Congress Catalog Card Number: 77-84871 Printed in the United States of America; vii-xiii Preface; xiv blank; xv Contents; xvi blank; xvii-xviii List of Illustrations; 1 section-title THE HERON AND THE ASTRONAUT; 2 blank; 3 chapter-title Cape Canaveral and Cape Kennedy text; 4-12 text; 2 leaves plates; 13-14 text; 15 chapter-title Night--The New Moon text; 16-18 text; 19 chapter-title Morning--"The Bird Perched for Flight" text; 20-23 text; 24 blank; 25 chapter-title Afternoon-- Merritt Island Refuge text; 26-28 text; 2 leaves plates; 29 text; 30 blank; 31 chapter-title Dialogue--Earth and Moon text; 32-37 text; 38 blank; 39 chapter-title Back to Earth text; 40-45 text; 46 blank; 47 section-title IMMERSION IN LIFE; 48 blank; 49-52 text; 2 leaves plates; 53-60 text; 2 leaves plates; 61-73 text; 74, 75, 76 blank; end pages, one confederate blue heavy paper; one white heavy paper.

+   +   +   +   +

Supplementary note:

Other publication of EARTH SHINE of noteworthy mention

   1969 London, Chatto & Windus

A9   BRING ME A UNICORN   1972
            Diaries and Letters of Anne Morrow Lindbergh
                            1922 - 1928

Issued in hard cover three-piece sky-blue linen cloth over upper

and lower boards; ultramarine linen cloth over spine with .05 cm.

overlap on boards. _/signature_/ Anne Morrow Lindbergh stamped in

imitation gold foil on upper board; 015-114180-0 stamped in

imitation gold foil on lower board; spine stamped in imitation

gold foil _/down, above_/ BRING ME A UNICORN _/down, below_/ Diaries

and Letters of Anne Morrow Lindbergh _/across_/ 1922 ⋮ _/rule_/ ⋮

1928 ⋮ _/design feature_/ ⋮ Harcourt ⋮ Brace ⋮ Jovanovich ⋮

/publisher's device/

Notes: Natural cream colored wove paper; ultramarine border and

letters on tan linings; all edges trimmed

Photographs on 24 pages coated paper; 8 pages between 38-39; 8

pages between 118-119; 8 pages between pages 198-199

COLLATION: 8° 8 signatures; 4° 2 signatures; stitched

PAGINATION: _/i-viii_/ ix-xi _/xii_/ xiii-xxv _/xxvi_/ _/1-2_/ 3-7 _/8-10_/

11 _/12-14_/ 15-16 _/17-18_/ 19-23 _/24-26_/ 27-61 _/62-64_/ 65-110

_/111-112_/ 113-249 _/250_/ 251-259 _/260-262_/

CONTENTS: Ultramarine border and letters on tan heavy end page;

i half-title; ii blank; iii Books by Anne Morrow Lindbergh; iv

blank; v title-page BRING ME A ⋮ UNICORN ⋮ /design feature7 ⋮
Diaries ⋮ and Letters ⋮ of ⋮ Anne Morrow Lindbergh ⋮ /design
feature7 ⋮ 1922 /rule7 1928 ⋮ A Helen and Kurt Wolff Book ⋮
Harcourt Brace Jovanovich, Inc., New York; vi Copyright ℮ 1971,
1972 by Anne Morrow Lindbergh ⋮ All rights reserved. ⋮ No part of
this publication may be reproduced ⋮ or transmitted in any form ⋮
or by any means, electronic or mechanical, ⋮ including photocopy,
recording, ⋮ or any information storage and retrieval system, ⋮
without permission in writing ⋮ from the publisher. ⋮ First
edition ⋮ ISBN 0-15-114180-0 ⋮ Library of Congress Catalog Card
Number: 71-182329 ⋮ Printed in the United States of America ⋮ B C
D E F ⋮ /publisher's device7 ⋮ The lines by James Stephens on page
45 are from "The Paps of Dana" ⋮ and are reprinted with permission
of The Macmillan Company, New ⋮ York; Mrs. Iris Wise; Macmillan
London and Basingstoke; and The ⋮ Macmillan Company of Canada Limited
from Collected Poems by James ⋮ Stephens, copyright 1915 by the
Macmillan Company, renewed 1943 by ⋮ James Stephens. John Masefield's
lines on page 109 are from "The Passing ⋮ Strange" and are reprinted
with the permission of The Macmillan Com- ⋮ pany, New York, and The
Society of Authors as the literary representative ⋮ of the Estate of
John Masefield, from Poems by John Masefield, copyright ⋮ 1920 by
John Masefield, renewed 1948 by John Masefield. The lines on ⋮
page 110 of Edgar Lee Master's "Alexander Throckmorton" are from ⋮
Spoon River Anthology, copyright 1915, 1916, 1942, 1944 by Edgar
Lee ⋮ Masters, and are reprinted by permission of Ellen C. Masters.
vii poem Everything today has been; viii blank; ix-x Acknowledgments;

xi <u>Editorial</u> <u>Note</u>; xii blank; xiii-xiv ILLUSTRATIONS; xx-xxv
INTRODUCTION; xxvi blank; 1 fly-title 1922; 2 blank; 3-7 text; 8
blank; 9 fly-title 1923; 10 blank; 11 text; 12 blank; 13 fly-title
1924; 14 blank; 15-16 text; 17 fly-title 1925; 18 blank; 19-23 text
/poem HEIGHT on pp. 22 and 23/; 24 blank; 25 fly-title 1926; 26
blank; 27-38 text; 8 pages photographs; 39-61 text; 62 blank; 63
fly-title 1927; 64 blank; 65-110 text; 111 fly-title 1928; 112
blank; 113-118 text; 8 pages photographs; 119-198 text; 8 pages
photographs; 199-249 text; 250 blank; 251-259 INDEX; 260-262
blank; ultramarine border and letters on tan heavy end page.

+   +   +   +   +

Supplementary notes:

Other publications of BRING ME A UNICORN <u>Diaries</u> <u>and</u> <u>Letters</u> <u>of</u>
<u>Anne</u> <u>Morrow</u> <u>Lindbergh</u> <u>1922</u> - <u>1928</u> of noteworthy mention

   1. 1972 Harcourt Brace Jovanovich, Book Club Edition

      1972 New American Library

      1972 G.K. Hall, Large Print Edition

      1972 Reader's Digest Condensed Books

   2. Translation:

      1972 German-München, R. Piper

   3. Excerpt:

      McCall Magazine 104 (June 1977): 118-119; 173-180

A10   HOUR OF GOLD, HOUR OF LEAD   1973
                Diaries and Letters of Anne Morrow Lindbergh
                              1929 - 1932

Issued in three-piece zinc-orange color linen cloth over boards;
spine ultramarine linen cloth over spine with .05 cm. overlap on
upper and lower boards. Upper board /signature/ Anne Morrow
Lindbergh stamped in imitation gold foil; lower board /ISBN/
0-15-142176-5 stamped in gold foil; spine stamped in imitation
gold foil /down, above/ HOUR OF GOLD, HOUR OF LEAD : /down, below/
Diaries and Letters of Anne Morrow Lindbergh; /across/ 1929 :
/rule/ : 1932 : /feature design/ : Harcourt : Brace : Jovanovich :
/publisher's device/
Notes: Natural cream colored wove paper; ultramarine border and
letters on zinc-orange lining paper; all edges trimmed
Photographs 2 leaves between pages 52-53; 2 leaves between pages
132-133; 2 leaves between pages 196-197; 2 leaves between pages
276-277

COLLATION: 8° 10 signatures; 4° 2 signatures; stitched

PAGINATION: /i-viii/ ix-xi /xii/ /1-2/ 3-12 /13-14/ 15-114
/115-116/ 117-147 /148-150/ 151-207 /208-210/ 211-217 /218-222/
223-325 /326/ 327-340

CONTENTS: Ultramarine border and letters on zinc-orange end page;
i half-title; ii blank; iii Books by Anne Morrow Lindbergh; iv
blank; v title-page HOUR OF GOLD, : HOUR OF LEAD : /design feature/
: Diaries : and Letters : of : Anne Morrow Lindbergh : /design

feature_7 ┊ 1929 - 1932 ┊ A Helen and Kurt Wolff Book ┊ Harcourt
Brace Jovanovich ┊ New York and London; vi Copyright ⊖ 1973 by
Anne Morrow Lindbergh ┊ All rights reserved. ┊ No part of this
publication may be reproduced ┊ or transmitted in any form ┊ or by
any means, electronic or mechanical, ┊ including photocopy,
recording, ┊ or any information storage and retrieval system, ┊
without permission in writing ┊ from the publisher. ┊ First
edition ┊ ISBN 0-15-142176-5 ┊ Library of Congress Catalog Card
Number: 72-88792 ┊ Printed in the United States of America ┊ B C D E
┊ ⎣publisher's device⎦ ┊ "Second Sowing," quoted on p. 219, is from
The Unicorn and Other Poems ┊ by Anne Morrow Lindbergh. Copyright
1948 by Anne Morrow Lindbergh. ┊ Reprinted by permission of
Pantheon Books, A Division of Random House, ┊ Inc. The verses on
p. 293 are from The Complete Poems of Emily Dickin- ┊ son, edited
by Thomas H. Johnson. Copyright 1929, ⊖ 1957 by Mary L. ┊ Hampson,
reprinted by permission of Little, Brown and Co. ┊ vii Editorial
Note; viii blank; ix-xi ILLUSTRATIONS; xii blank; 1 sectional title-
page HOUR OF GOLD; 2 blank; 3-12 Introduction; 13 fly-title 1929;
14 blank; 15-52 text; 2 leaves photographs; 53-114 text; 115 fly-
title 1930; 116 blank; 117-132 text; 2 leaves photographs; 133-147
text; 148 blank; 149 fly-title 1931; 150 blank; 151-196 text; 2
leaves photographs; 197-207 text; 208 blank; 209 sectional title-
page HOUR OF LEAD; 210 blank; 211-217 Introduction; 218 blank; 219
poem Second Sowing; 220 blank; 221 fly-title 1932; 222 blank; 223-
276 text; 2 leaves photographs; 277-325 text; 326 blank; 327-340
INDEX; ultramarine border and letters on zinc-orange end page.

+   +   +   +   +

Supplementary notes:

Other publications of HOUR OF GOLD, HOUR OF LEAD Diaries and

Letters of Anne Morrow Lindbergh 1929 - 1932 of noteworthy mention

1. 1973 Harcourt Brace Jovanovich, Book Club Edition

    1973 New American Library

    1974 G.K. Hall, Large Print Edition

2. Translations:

    1973 German-München, R. Piper and Company

3. Excerpt:

    "Lindbergh Nightmare." Time Magazine 101 (February 5, 1973): 35

A11   LOCKED ROOMS AND OPEN DOORS   1974
            Diaries and Letters of Anne Morrow Lindbergh
                         1933 - 1935

Issued in hard cover three-piece seashell linen cloth over upper and

lower boards; ultramarine linen cloth on spine with .05 cm. overlap

on boards; upper board /signature7 Anne Morrow Lindbergh stamped

in imitation gold foil; lower board /ISBN7 0-15-152958-2 stamped

in imitation gold foil; spine stamped in imitation gold foil /down,

above7 LOCKED ROOMS AND OPEN DOORS ⋮ /down, below7 Diaries and

Letters of Anne Morrow Lindbergh; /across7 1933 ⋮ /rule7 ⋮ 1935 ⋮

Harcourt ⋮ Brace ⋮ Jovanovich ⋮ /publisher's device7

Notes: Natural cream colored wove paper; ultramarine border and

letters on tan lining papers; all edges trimmed

Photographs 2 leaves between pages 70-71; 2 leaves between pages
134-135; 2 leaves between pages 198-199; 2 leaves between pages
262-263

COLLATION: 8° 12 signatures; stitched

PAGINATION: /i-vi/ vii /viii/ ix-xi /xii/ xiii-xxvi /1-2/ 3-183
/184-186/ 187-232 /233-234/ 235-352 /353-358/

CONTENTS: Ultramarine border and letters on verso upper and recto
lower tan heavy end papers; i half-title; ii blank; iii Books by
Anne Morrow Lindbergh; iv blank; v title-page LOCKED ROOMS : AND :
OPEN DOORS : /design feature/ : Diaries : and Letters : of :
Anne Morrow Lindbergh : /design feature/ : 1933 : /rule/ : 1935 :
A Helen and Kurt Wolff Book : Harcourt Brace Jovanovich : New York
and London : /publisher's device/ : vi Copyright © 1974 by Anne
Morrow Lindbergh : All rights reserved. : No part of this
publication may be reproduced : or transmitted in any form : or by
any means, electronic or mechanical, : including photocopy,
recording, : or any information storage and retrieval system, :
without permission in writing : from the publisher. : Printed in
the United States of America : Library of Congress Cataloging in
Publication Data : Lindbergh, Anne (Morrow) 1906- : Locked rooms
and open doors: 1933-1935. : "A Helen and Kurt Wolff book." :
I. Lindbergh, Anne (Morrow) 1906- I. Title. : PS3523.^{I}516Z52
818'.5'209 /B/ 73-16152 : ISBN 0-15-152958-2 : First edition :
B C D E : John Masefield's lines on page 229 are from "The Passing
Strange" and are : reprinted with the permission of The Macmillan

Company, New York, and ⋮ The Society of Authors as the literary
representative of the Estate of John ⋮ Masefield, from Poems by
John Masefield, copyright 1920 by John Masefield, ⋮ renewed 1948 by
John Masefield. Edna St. Vincent Millay's lines on page 322 ⋮ are
from Sonnet 36 in Fatal Interview and are reprinted with the
permission of ⋮ Norma Millay Ellis, from Collected Poems, copyright
1931-1959 by Edna ⋮ St. Vincent Millay and Norma Millay Ellis,
published by Harper & Row.; vii Editorial Note; viii blank; ix-xi
ILLUSTRATIONS; xii blank; xiii-xxvi INTRODUCTION; 1 fly-title 1933;
2 blank; 3-70 text; 8 pages photographs; 71-134 text; 8 pages
photographs; 135-183 text; 184 blank; 185 fly-title 1934; 186 blank;
187-198 text; 8 pages photographs; 199-232 text; 233 fly-title
1935; 234 blank; 235-262 text; 8 pages photographs; 263-336 text;
337-352 INDEX; 353-358 blank; ultramarine border and letters on
tan heavy end papers.

                +   +   +   +   +

Supplementary Notes:
Other publications of LOCKED ROOMS AND OPEN DOORS Diaries and
Letters of Anne Morrow Lindbergh 1933 - 1935 of noteworthy mention
   1. 1974 G.K. Hall, Large Print Edition
   2. Translation:
      1975 German-München, R. Piper and Company

A12   THE FLOWER AND THE NETTLE   1976
                 Diaries and Letters of Anne Morrow Lindbergh
                              1936 - 1939

Issued in hard cover three-piece binding; white linen cloth over

upper and lower boards; ultramarine linen cloth on spine with .05 cm.

overlap on boards; upper board /signature/ Anne Morrow Lindbergh

stamped in imitation gold foil; lower board /ISBN/ 0-15-131501-9

stamped in imitation gold foil; spine stamped in imitation gold

foil /down, above/ THE FLOWER AND THE NETTLE : /down, below/

Diaries and Letters of Anne Morrow Lindbergh; /across/ 1936 :

/rule/ : 1939 : /design feature/ : Harcourt : Brace : Jovanovich :

/publisher's device/

Notes: Cream color wove paper; ultramarine border and letters on

Persian orange heavy lining papers; all edges trimmed

Photographs 2 leaves between pages 66-67; 4 leaves between pages

162-163; 2 leaves between pages 450-451

COLLATION: 8° 20 signatures; stitched

PAGINATION: /i-viii/ ix-xi /xii/ xiii-xxix /xxx/ /1-2/ 3-119

/120-122/ 123-193 /194-196/ 197-480 /481-482/ 483-605 /606-610/

CONTENTS: Persian orange heavy end paper; i half-title; ii blank;

iii Books by Anne Morrow Lindbergh; iv blank; v title-page THE

FLOWER : AND THE NETTLE : /design feature/ : Diaries : and

Letters : of : Anne Morrow Lindbergh : /design feature/ : 1936

/rule/ 1939 : A Helen and Kurt Wolff Book : Harcourt Brace

Jovanovich : New York and London : /publisher's device/;

vi Copyright © 1976 by Anne Morrow Lindbergh ⋮ All rights
reserved. ⋮ No part of this publication may be reproduced ⋮ or
transmitted in any form ⋮ or by any means, electronic or
mechanical, ⋮ including photocopy, recording, ⋮ or any information
storage and retrieval system, ⋮ without permission in writing ⋮
from the publisher. ⋮ Printed in the United States of America ⋮
Library of Congress Cataloging in Publication Data ⋮ Lindbergh,
Anne Morrow, 1906- ⋮ The flower and the nettle. ⋮ Continuation of
the author's Locked rooms and open doors. ⋮ "A Helen and Kurt Wolff
book." ⋮ Includes index. ⋮ I. Lindbergh, Anne Morrow, 1906- --
Diaries. ⋮ 2. Lindbergh, Anne Morrow, 1906- --Correspondence. I.
Title. ⋮ PS3523.I516Z516 1976 818'.5'209 /B/ 75-25708 ⋮
ISBN 0-15-131501-9 ⋮ First edition ⋮ BCDE ⋮ W.B. Yeats's lines on
page 545 are from "Coole Park, 1929" from The ⋮ Collected Poems
and are reprinted by permission of Macmillan Publishing ⋮ Co.,
Inc., M.B. Yeats, Miss Anne Yeats, and Macmillan of London and ⋮
Basingstoke, copyright 1933 by Macmillan Publishing Co., Inc.,
renewed ⋮ 1961 by Bertha Georgie Yeats.; vii Editorial Note;
viii blank; ix-xi ILLUSTRATIONS; xii blank; xiii-xxviii
INTRODUCTION; xxix Introduction /footnotes/; xxx blank; 1 fly-
title 1936; 2 blank; 3-66 text; 8 pages photographs; 67-119 text;
120 blank; 121 fly-title 1937; 122 blank; 123-162 text; 16 pages
photographs; 163-193 text; 194 blank; 195 fly-title 1938; 196 blank;
197-450 text; 8 pages photographs; 451-480 text; 481 fly-title
1939; 482 blank; 483-582 text; 583-605 INDEX; 606-610 blank;
Persian·orange heavy end paper.

A13   THE JOURNEY NOT THE ARRIVAL   1978

Issued in three-piece hard cover binding; sapphire blue paper
over upper and lower boards; design feature stamped in imitation
gold foil on upper board; spine Ismic blue linen cloth with 3.03 cm.
overlap on boards; spine stamped in gold imitation foil /down/
Anne Morrow Lindbergh THE JOURNEY NOT THE ARRIVAL /publisher's
design/ HARCOURT BRACE JOVANOVICH

Notes: Saint-Gilles "Blanc" handmade paper; sapphire blue heavy
paper lining on boards; head and foot edges trimmed; fore-edges
deckle-edged

COLLATION: 2° 2 signatures; stitched

PAGINATION: /i-iv/ 1-11 /12/

CONTENTS: Sapphire blue heavy blue end page; i front matter; ii
blank; iii title-page Anne Morrow Lindbergh : /decoration feature/ :
THE JOURNEY : NOT THE ARRIVAL : HARCOURT BRACE JOVANOVICH : New
York and London : /publisher's device/; iv Copyright © 1978 by
Anne Morrow Lindbergh : All rights reserved. : The paper, Saint-
Gilles "Blanc," is handmade by Papeterie Saint-Gilles, : at
Saint-Joseph-de-la-Rive, Quebec, Canada. : The book is printed in
the United States of America by A.Colish, Inc., : Mount Vernon,
N.Y., and bound by A.Horowitz & Sons, Fairfield, N.J.; 1-11 text;
12 blank; sapphire blue heavy end page.

            +   +   +   +   +

Supplementary Note: THE JOURNEY NOT THE ARRIVAL given as a speech
at Smith College in Northampton, Massachusetts, 1978.

B

ARTICLES, ESSAYS, PREFACE

B1 "Flying Around the North Atlantic." <u>National Geographic</u>, 66
    (Sept. 1934) 259-337.

B2 "Adventurous Writing." <u>Review of Wind, Sand and Stars</u> by
    Antoine de Saint Exupery. <u>The Saturday Review</u>, 20
    (14 Oct. 1939) 8-9.

B3 "Prayer for Peace." <u>Reader's Digest</u>, 36 (Jan. 1940) 1-8.

B4 "Reaffirmation." <u>Atlantic</u>, 167 (June 1941) 681-6.

B5 "The Most Unforgettable Character I've Met." <u>Reader's Digest</u>,
    50 (Jan. 1947) 1-4, 171-4.

B6 "The Flame of Europe." <u>Reader's Digest</u>, 52 (Jan. 1948) 141-6.

B7 "One Starts at Zero." <u>Reader's Digest</u>, 52 (Feb. 1948) 73-5.

B8 "Anywhere In Europe." Harper's /magazine7, 196 (April 1948)
    300-2.

B9 "Airliner to Europe." <u>Harper's</u> /magazine7, 197 (Sept. 1948)
    43-7.

B10 "Our Lady of Risk." <u>Life</u>, 29 (10 July 1950) 80-6, 88, 91.

B11 Adams, James Donald, ed. "The Man Who Lived Twice: Edward
    Sheldon." <u>Triumph Over Odds An Anthology of Man's Unconquerable</u>
    <u>Spirit</u>. New York: Duell, Sloan and Pearce, 1957, pp. 435-441.

B12 Long, Haniel. /Preface7 <u>Spring Returns</u>. New York: Pantheon,
    1958, pp. v-ix.

B13 "As I See Our First Lady." <u>Look</u>, 28 (19 May 1964) 100, 102,
    105-6, 108, 110.

B14 "Immersion In Life: Journey to East Africa." <u>Life</u>, 61
    (21 Oct. 1966) 88-90, 92, 94, 98.

B15   "Discovery and Renewal From a Family Safari to East Africa."
       Reader's Digest, 90 (Jan. 1967) 37-43.

B16   "The Heron and the Astronaut." Life, 66 (28 Feb. 1969) 14-27.

B17   "Harmony With the Life Around Us." Good Housekeeping, 171
       (July 1970) 62-3, 150-3.

C

POEMS

1928

C1   "Height." <u>Scribner's Magazine</u>, 83 (Apr. 1928) 409.

1929

C2   "Height." <u>Outlook and Independent</u>, 151 (27 Feb. 1929) 335.

C3   "Caprice," "A Certain Woman," "A Letter With A Foreign Stamp,"
     "Unicorn." <u>Literary Digest</u>, 100 (9 Mar. 1929) 42-3, 46.

C4   "Remembrance." <u>Literary Digest</u>, 100 (16 Mar. 1929) 29.

1934

C5   Markham, Edwin, ed. "Height." <u>The Book of American Poetry</u>.
     New York: William H. Wise & Co., 1934, p. 822.

1937

C6   Longworth, Alice Roosevelt and Theodore Roosevelt, eds.
     "Caprice." <u>The Desk Drawer Anthology Poems for the American
     People</u>. Freeport, New York: Books for Libraries Press,
     1937, p. 192.

1939

C7   "No Harvest Ripening." <u>The Saturday Review of Literature</u>, 21
     (18 Nov. 1939) 10.

C8   "Security." <u>The Saturday Review of Literature</u>, 21
     (16 Dec. 1939) 8.

1940

C9   "Prayer for Peace." Reader's Digest, 36 (Jan. 1940) 1-8.

C10   "Alms," "Elegy Under the Stars," "Visitation." Atlantic,
      165 (Apr. 1940) 456-7.

C11   "A Final Cry," "Testament." Atlantic, 167, (Mar. 1941) 338-9.

1947

C12   Songs for Flying: "Closing In," "Growing up," "The Trolls."
      Atlantic, 180 (July 1947) 36.

C13   Two Poems for November: "All Saints' Day, "Burning Tree."
      Atlantic, 180 (4 Nov. 1947) 122.

1948

C14   "Second Sowing." Atlantic, 182 (Aug. 1948) 70.

1950

C15   "Winter Tree." Atlantic, 185 (Mar. 1950) 46.

1951

C16   "The Man and The Child." Atlantic, 187 (Feb. 1951) 29.

C17   "Within the Wave." Atlantic, 188 (Oct. 1951) 38.

C18   "Space." Atlantic, 188 (Nov. 1951) 35.

C19   "The Stone." Atlantic, 189 (Jan. 1952) 44.

1952

C20   Lamont, Corliss, ed. "Testament." Man Answers Death
      An Anthology of Poetry. Freeport, New York: Books for
      Libraries Press, 1952, p. 120.

C21 "A Leaf, A Flower, and A Stone." Atlantic, 190 (Oct. 1952) 52.

1954

C22 "Broken Shell." Atlantic, 193 (Jan. 1954) 64.

C23 "Back to the Islands." Atlantic, 193 (Mar. 1954) 66.

1955

C24 "Bare Tree." Atlantic, 195 (Mar. 1955) 56.

1956

C25 "Two Citadels." Ladies' Home Journal, 73 (Aug. 1956) 120.

C26 "Even." Ladies' Home Journal, 73 (Sept. 1956) 14.

C27 "Revisitation." Vogue, 128 (15 Sept. 1956) 122-3.

C28 "Dogwood." Ladies' Home Journal, 73 (Oct. 1956) 110.

1957

C29 "Mid-summer." Atlantic, 200 (Dec. 1957) 44.

1974

C30 A Quartet of Lyrics: "Alms," "Interior Tree," "Space,"

     "Two Citadels," The Saturday Evening Post, 246

     (Jan./Feb. 1974) 22.

II.

WRITINGS ABOUT A.M. LINDBERGH

D

ARTICLES ABOUT A.M. LINDBERGH

D1   "In This Romantic World." <u>Outlook</u> <u>and</u> <u>Independent</u>, 100

     (27 Feb. 1929) 335.

     Reprints 1928 <u>Scribner's</u> poem "Height"; announces engagement

     of Anne Morrow Lindbergh and Charles Augustus Lindbergh.

D2   "Anne Morrow Makes It 'We Three'." <u>The</u> <u>Literary</u> <u>Digest</u>, 100

     (9 Mar. 1929) 38, 43, 46.

     Praises mastery of writing.

D3   Denny, Harold Norman. "Lindy and Anne Wed!" <u>The</u> <u>New</u> <u>Republic</u>,

     59 (26 June 1929) 145-7.

     Comments on desire for privacy.

D4   "Joins Girls' Glider Club." <u>The</u> <u>New</u> <u>York</u> <u>Times</u>, 79 (17 Feb. 1930) 7.

     Announces Glider Club membership.

D5   "Husband-and-Wife Teams in the Flying Game." <u>The</u> <u>Literary</u>

     <u>Digest</u>, 105 (12 Apr. 1930) 39-40.

     Reveals AML's flying teacher is C.A. Lindbergh.

D6   "Radio Appeal for Chinese Flood Relief." <u>The</u> <u>New</u> <u>York</u> <u>Times</u>, 80

     (22 Feb. 1932) 18.

     Devotes two columns to radio speech.

D7   "Personality On The Air." <u>The</u> <u>New</u> <u>York</u> <u>Times</u>, 81 (20 Mar. 1932) 14.

     Notices lack of speaking accent.

D8   "Lindbergh Tour Delayed Six Months." <u>The</u> <u>New</u> <u>York</u> <u>Times</u>, 83

     (6 Dec. 1933) 26.

     Reports time devoted to surveys.

D9   "Mrs. Lindbergh Is the Third Woman to Fly Across the Atlantic

      in an Airplane." "Lindberghs Fly to Brazil From Africa in 16

      Hours." "Lindbergh Radio Reported Often." The New York Times,

      83 (7 Dec. 1933) 3.

D10   "The Lindberghs Blaze Another Trail." The Literary Digest, 116

      (16 Dec. 1933) 7.

D11   "Anne Lindbergh: Roaming Far Skies, Longs for Home." Newsweek,

      2 (16 Dec. 1933) 16.

      Finds manner of expression "distinguished."

D12   Lyman, Laureen D. "Lindberghs Back Safely After 30,000-Mile

      Flight." The New York Times, 83 (20 Dec. 1933) 1.

D13   "Lindberghs Saw 21 Nations on Trip." The New York Times, 83 (20 Dec.

      1933) 1.

D14   "Cross of Honor Awarded to Mrs. Lindbergh; Flag Association

      Will Present It Today." The New York Times, 83 (25 Dec. 1933) 1.

D15   W.M.H. "At the Observation Post; Lindberghs Complete Their

      29,000-Mile Tour." The Literary Digest, 116 (30 Dec. 1933) 12.

D16   "Hubbard Gold Medal by National Geographic Society Awarded to

      Her; First Woman to Receive Medal." The New York Times, 83

      (31 Jan. 1934) 19.

D17   "The Co-Pilot." The New York Times, 83 (1 Feb. 1934) 18.

      Regards AML's account of travels as overall contribution to

      schools' geographic study.

D18   "To Honor Mrs. Lindbergh Gold Medal for Meritorious Radio

      Service, by Veteran Wireless Operators Association." The

      New York Times, 83 (24 Feb. 1934) 11.

D19   Sussman, L.   "Portrait."   Pictorial Review, 35 (Apr. 1934) 78.
      Not seen.

D20   "Eskimos Making Costume for Mrs. Lindbergh."   The New York Times,
      83 (1 Apr. 1934) 1.

D21   "Awarded Harmon National Trophy by International League of
      Aviators."   The New York Times, 83 (22 Apr. 1934) 6.

D22   "Portrait."   The New York Times, 83 (27 May 1934) 4.
      Not seen.

D23   "The Society Awards Hubbard Medal To Anne Morrow Lindbergh."
      National Geographic Magazine, 65 (June 1934) 790-4.

D24   "Anne Lindbergh, In a Gay Humor, Writes Secrets of World Flights."
      The New York Times, 83 (30 Aug. 1934) 21.
      Feels narrative needs no cutting.

D25   "Mrs. Lindbergh Pens Book On Air Junket."   The New York Times,
      83 (14 May 1935) 23.

D26   "About Her Travels."   The New York Times, 84 (19 May 1935) 2.
      Review of North to the Orient. Cheers AML's new form of writing.

D27   "Books for the Summer Months."   The New York Times, 84 (16 June
      1935) 18, 20.
      Announces North to the Orient as a book of "adventurous flight."

D28   "Receives Honorary Degree, /Master of Arts/ Smith College."
      The New York Times, 84 (18 June 1935) 15.

D29   Review of North to the Orient. Wisconsin Library Bulletin, 31
      (8 July 1935) 83.
      Says libraries would do well to acquire this book.

D30   Review of <u>North to the Orient</u>. <u>New York New Technical Books</u>,

      20 (July 1935) 27.

      Not seen.

D31   Review of <u>North to the Orient</u>. <u>Cleveland Open Shelf</u>,

      (Aug. 1935) 15.

      Not seen.

D32   Review of <u>North to the Orient</u>. <u>Christian Century</u>, 52

      (14 Aug. 1935) 1039.

      Considers book important because of versatility.

D33   Review of <u>North to the Orient</u>. <u>Christian Science Monitor</u>,

      (14 Aug. 1935) 11.

      Not seen.

D34   Gannett, Lewis. <u>New York Herald Tribune</u>, (15 Aug. 1935) 15.

      Review of <u>North to the Orient</u>. Points out AML's effectiveness

      as a writer.

D35   Bayley, Gertrude. <u>Boston Transcript</u>, (17 Aug. 1935) 3.

      Review of <u>NO</u>. Notes simplicity in story an asset.

D36   Butcher, Fanny. <u>Chicago Daily Tribune</u>, (17 Aug. 1935) 8.

      Review of <u>NO</u>. Describes as a revealing travel book.

D37   Loveman, Amy. "The Seeing Eye." <u>Saturday Review of Literature</u>,

      12 (17 Aug. 1935) 6.

      States maps in <u>North to the Orient</u> contribute to this "charming

      book."

D38   Nicolson, Harold. <u>Newsweek</u>, 6 (17 Aug. 1935) 36.

      Characterizes AML skillful as a writer and a pilot.

D39 Niles, Blair. Books, (18 Aug. 1935) 1.

Sees NO as good story as well as historic record.

D40 Poore, C.G. "The Lindbergh Flight to Tokyo." The New York

Times Book Review, 6 (18 Aug. 1935) 1, 4, 14.

Chooses AML's "light, acute, candid" style of NO superior

to a technical reporting treatment.

D41 "Anne Lindbergh's Book A Hit." Publishers Weekly, 128

(24 Aug. 1935) 508.

Notes national endorsement of NO.

D42 Review of North to the Orient. Springfield Republican,

(25 Aug. 1935) 5.

Not seen.

D43 Review of North to the Orient. Commonweal, 22 (30 Aug. 1935) 432.

Conjectures about the motivation of the writer.

D44 Review of North to the Orient. Pratt Institute, (Autumn 1935) 28.

Not seen.

D45 Review of North to the Orient. The Booklist, 32 (Sept. 1935) 12.

Considers style pleasant and unstilted.

D46 Chamberlain, John. "The World In Books." Current History, 43

(Oct. 1935) 6-7.

Maintains AML has a "sense of humor."

D47 Review of North to the Orient. Geographic Review, 25

(Oct. 1935) 704.

Aware of geographical contribution.

D48 Review of North to the Orient. Horn Book Magazine, 11

(Oct. 1935) 299.

Declares book has universal appeal.

D49   Review of <u>NO</u>. <u>Review of Reviews</u>, 92 (Oct. 1935) 5.

      Approves book for readers enthusiastic about aviation.

D50   E.J.C. <u>Catholic World</u>, 142 (Oct. 1935) 122.

      Comments on author's interest in the Orient.

D51   Walton, E.H. <u>Forum</u>, 94 (Oct. 1935) 6.

      Praises writing style.

D52   Weeks, Edward. <u>Atlantic Bookshelf</u>, 156 (Oct. 1935) 22.

      Thinks that author should continue writing.

D53   Beard, Mary R. <u>New Republic</u>, 84 (2 Oct. 1935) 222.

      Questions feminism, in <u>NO</u>.

D54   Review of <u>North to the Orient</u>. <u>The Times</u> /London/ <u>Literary</u>
      <u>Supplement</u>, (3 Oct. 1935) 607.

      Presents AML's aeroplane as a "magic carpet."

D55   Richardson, M.L. <u>New Statesman & Nation</u>, 10 (12 Oct. 1935)
      526.

      Points out AML's skill in communicating a "definite sensation
      of flight" in <u>North to the Orient</u>.

D56   Scoggin, Margaret C. <u>The Library Journal</u>, 60 (1 Nov. 1935)
      825.

      Agrees with AML's statement: "Magic of Mystery."

D57   Review of <u>North to the Orient</u>. <u>The Booklist</u>, 32 (Dec. 1935) 117.

      Impressed with method of communicating ideas.

D58   Review of <u>North to the Orient</u>. <u>The Spectator</u>, 155
      (6 Dec. 1935) 952, 954.

      Characterizes the book as a "quality of adventure" record.

D59   "Mrs. Catt Names Ten 'First Women'." The New York Times,
      83 (10 Dec. 1935) 29.
      States that selection of AML was "principally as the author
      of a successful book."

D60   "Forms Education Foundation." The New York Times,
      (20 Dec. 1935) 15.

D61   "Portrait of Anne Morrow Lindbergh." National Geographic
      Magazine, 69 (Jan. 1936) 136-7.
      Refers to gold medal.

D62   Ross, David Allan. Independent Woman, 15 (Jan. 1936) 11, 26.
      Proclaims NO "a piece of literary craftsmanship."

D63   Villard, Oswald Garrison. "Issues and Men The Lindberghs
      Leave." Nation, 142 (8 Jan. 1936) 35.
      Gives a dissertation on influence of media.

D64   "Four Best-selling Personalities." The Literary Digest,
      121 (11 Jan. 1936) 28.
      Comments on "direct manner."

D65   "Portrait." Publishers Weekly, 129 (16 May 1936) 1948-9.
      Announces NO "Most distinguished general nonfiction" book.

D66   Review of North to the Orient. The Booklist, 32 (June 1936) 298.
      Views writing style as straightforward.

D67   Coffin, Robert P. Tristram. "Looking At Life From The Sky."
      Yale Review, 25 (Winter 1936) 390.
      Refers to the usefulness of facts in NO.

D68   Chase, M.E. Commonweal, 28 (14 Oct. 1938) 645.
      Discovers coruscation in Listen! the Wind.

D69 Review of _Listen! the Wind_. _The Booklist_, 35 (15 Oct. 1938) 62.

Says the book recommends itself.

D70 Fadiman, Clifton. _The New Yorker_, 14 (15 Oct. 1938) 92.

Values _LW_ for "aeronautical history" as well as a work of "art."

D71 Loveman, Amy. _Saturday Review of Literature_, 18 (15 Oct. 1938) 5.

Lauds style and content of _LW_.

D72 Review of _Listen! the Wind_. _Springfield Republican_, (16 Oct. 1938)

Not seen.

D73 Soskin, William. Review of _LW_. _Books_, (16 Oct. 1938) 1.

Elaborates on AML's writing artistry.

D74 Woods, Katherine. "A Tale of Pioneers in the Air." _The New
York Times Book Review_, (16 Oct. 1938) 1, 29.

Emphasizes the fact-full and action-full account of _LW_.

D75 "The Flying Colonel's Lady." _Newsweek_, 12 (17 Oct. 1938) 35-6.

Holds that _LW_ is more than a "flight log"; it is a work of

a "poet."

D76 M.S. Review of _LW_. _Christian Science Monitor_, (19 Oct. 1938) 11.

Praises writing style.

D77 Pitts, Rebecca. _New Republic_, 96 (19 Oct. 1938) 315.

Evaluates Part I of _LW_ "bogged down with static description"

and Part II lifting "cleanly into suspense."

D78 "Take Off." _Time_, 32 (24 Oct. 1938) 70.

Compares _North to the Orient_ with _Listen! the Wind_.

D79 Review of _LW_. _Christian Century_, 55 (26 Oct. 1938) 1298.

Praises literary ability.

D80 Garnett, David. New Statesman & Nation, 16 (29 Oct. 1938) 690.

Confesses that after reading AML's first book, he likes

"women better than men."

D81 Review of Listen! the Wind. Cleveland Open Shelf, (Nov. 1938) 18.

Not seen.

D82 Review of Listen! the Wind. Wisconsin Library Bulletin, 34

(Nov. 1938) 178.

Respects the "delicate touch" of the book.

D83 Elting, M.L. The Forum and Century, 6 (Nov. 1938) 6.

Ranks writing in Listen! the Wind more subtle, "more mature"

than in North to the Orient.

D84 Weeks, Edward. Atlantic, (Nov. 1938).

Wishes Listen! the Wind were "longer."

D85 Scoggin, Margaret C. The Library Journal, 63 (1 Nov. 1938) 828.

Classifies Listen! the Wind as "poetry and drama."

D86 "Down the Corridors of Flight." The Times /London/ Literary

Supplement, (12 Nov. 1938) 729.

Directs eyes to the realism and "poetry" in Listen! the Wind.

D87 De V.R., F.A. Manchester Guardian, (25 Nov. 1938) 7.

Sees writing in LW as outgrowth of interesting life experiences.

D88 B.L.C. Catholic World, 148 (Dec. 1938) 368.

Perceives pleasure for readers of LW.

D89 Kellogg, F.L. Survey Graphic, 27 (Dec. 1938) 626.

Suggests careful reading of LW.

D90 Review of Listen! the Wind. The Booklist, 35 (15 Dec. 1938) 145.

Relates problems associated with aviation.

D91   Review of Listen! the Wind. Horn Book Magazine, 15
      (Jan. 1939) 43.
      Acknowledges LW will interest "older young people."

D92   Copithorn, B. Churchman, 153 (1 Jan. 1939) 20.
      Recommends LW for universal appeal.

D93   Review of Listen! the Wind. The Booklist, 35 (15 Feb. 1939) 211.
      Recommends book for "poetic quality."

D94   "Book, Listen! the Wind Wins American Booksellers Association
      Award." The New York Times, (15 Feb. 1939) 14.

D95   "Portrait." Publishers Weekly, 135 (18 Feb. 1939) 781.
      Announcement of LW being awarded "Favorite Non-Fiction."

D96   "Rochester Honor To Mrs. Lindbergh." The New York Times,
      88 (20 June 1939) 14.

D97   Lamont, W.H.F. "Comparison of With Malice Toward Some and
      Listen! the Wind." Educational Review, 60 (21 Oct. 1939) 109-121.

D98   Review of Listen! the Wind. Pratt Institute, (Winter 1939) 26.
      Not seen.

D99   Brackman, Robert. Magazine of Art, 33 (Jan. 1940) 43.
      Comments on "penetration into character" of AML in WF.

D100 Review of The Wave of the Future. Cleveland Open Shelf,
      (Oct. 1940) 17.
      Not seen.

D101 Gannett, Lewis. Boston Transcript, (4 Oct. 1940) 11.
      Judges words written in WF by a "poet, an artist."

D102 "Footnotes on Headliners." The New York Times, (6 Oct. 1940) 2.
      Announces The Wave of the Future as a "discussion of the
      American position in a revolutionary world."

D103 Review of The Wave of the Future. Springfield Republican,
      (6 Oct. 1940) 7.
      Calls work vague.

D104 Review of WF. The New Yorker, 16 (12 Oct. 1940) 103.
      Refers to AML's method to fight totalitarianism.

D105 Marshall, Margaret. Nation, 151 (12 Oct. 1940) 330.
      Doubts message in WF.

D106 "Mrs. Lindbergh Speaks Out." Time, 36 (14 Oct. 1940) 31.
      Recognizes coherent design in WF.

D107 Edman, Irwin. Books, (20 Oct. 1940) 2.
      Critizes ambiguity in WF.

D108 Review of The Wave of the Future. Christian Century, 57
      (30 Oct. 1940) 1334-5.
      Ranks AML's affirmative stand notable.

D109 Weeks, Edward. Atlantic, (Nov. 1940).
      Points out opposing qualities for readers of WF.

D110 J.D.A. The New York Times Book Review, (3 Nov. 1940) 2, 18.
      Challenges "dogmatic" minds to read WF for the "provocative"
      message.

D111 Boothe, Clare. Current History, 52 (7 November 1940) 3-5.
      Extols prose in WF.

D112 M.W. Christian Science Monitor, (23 Nov. 1940) 11.
      Doubts merit of style without substance in WF.

D113 Review of The Wave of the Future. Current History & Forum,
      52 (26 Nov. 1940) 32.
      Predicts debates about book.

D114 Angell, Norman. Review of The Wave of the Future. Survey
      Graphic, 29 (Nov. 1940) 558-9.

      Concludes book is work of a "poet, perhaps of a mystic."

D115 Review of The Wave of the Future. Wisconsin Library Bulletin,
      36 (Dec. 1940) 166.

      Comments on some statements made in book.

D116 Block, Leon Bryce. Living Age, 359 (Dec. 1940) 384.

      Censures content of WF and at the same time, applauds the

      book for being "beautifully written."

D117 Review of The Wave of the Future. The Booklist, 37 (15 Dec.
      1940) 151.

      Observes some statements imprecise.

D118 Review of The Wave of the Future. Catholic World, 152 (Jan.
      1940) 508.

      Depicts presence of "literary style."

D119 Friedrich, Carl Joachim. Atlantic, 167 (Jan. 1941) 33-5.
      Argues that AML's analysis is incorrect and incomplete in WF.

D120 Grube, Gwenyth. Canadian Forum, 20 (Jan. 1941) 322.
      Assesses thesis in WF as "strange."

D121 Berlin, Mrs. Irving. The New York Times, (6 Jan. 1941) 6.
      Castigates book WF as German "propaganda."

D122 "Topics of The Times." The New York Times, (7 Jan. 1941) 22.
      Complains about the "spirit of fatalism" in WF.

D123 "Portrait." Life, 10 (20 Jan. 1941) 26.
      Reports on popularity of WF.

D124   "Wave of the Future to Be Subject of Italian Professor's
       /Guide Manacorda7 Lecture." The New York Times, 90 (3 Apr.
       1941) 11.

D125   "Ickes Offers A List of Nazi 'Tools' Here." The New York Times,
       90 (14 Apr. 1941) 19.
       Employs parallelism: The Wave of the Future, and the "bible of
       every American Nazi ... appeaser."

D126   Shaw, Abraham D., Rabbi. The New York Times, 90 (27 Apr. 1941) 23.
       Expresses strong disapproval of WF.

D127   "53 Women Named As Leaders of Sex." The New York Times, 90
       (9 May 1941) 17.
       AML praised by General Women's Clubs Federation.

D128   Thompson, Dorothy. Fortnightly, 155 (June 1941) 546-554.
       Disagrees with AML's assessment of the future in WF.

D129   Ickes, Harold L. The New York Times, 90 (15 July 1941) 13.
       Condemns AML for WF.

D130   Adams Jean and Margaret Kimball, in collaboration with Jeanette
       Eaton. "Anne Lindbergh Listen! The Poet." Heroines Of The Sky.
       Garden City, New York: Doubleday, Doran & Company, Inc., 1942,
       pp. 214-235.
       Impressed with AML's words, both in prose and poetry.

D131   White, E.B. "The Wave Of The Future." One Man's Meat.
       New York and Evanston: Harper & Row, Publishers, 1944,
       pp. 203-210.
       Implies what could be: Il y a fagots et fagots; quot homines
       tot sententiae.

D132   Review of Steep Ascent. Cleveland Open Shelf, (Mar. 1944) 8.
       Not seen.

D133   Review of Steep Ascent. Special Libraries, 35 (Mar. 1944) 101.
       Values comprehensive benefits of book.

D134   Review of Steep Ascent. Kirkus Reviews, 12 (1 Mar. 1944) 101.
       Impressed with spiritual message in book.

D135   Boyle, F.A. The Library Journal, 69 (15 Mar. 1944) 262.
       Glows with praise for SA.

D136   Loveman, Amy. Saturday Review of Literature, 27 (18 Mar.
       1944) 12.
       Recommends SA to former readers of North to the Orient and
       Listen! the Wind.

D137   Marindin, Eleanor. Springfield Republican, (19 Mar. 1944) 7.
       Review of SA. Not seen.

D138   North, Sterling. Book Week, (19 Mar. 1944) 2.
       Portrays SA "introspective in tone."

D139   Sancton, Thomas. Weekly Book Review, (19 Mar. 1944) 4.
       Suggests that there is a "towering introspection" in SA.

D140   Sherman, Beatrice. The New York Times Book Review, (19 Mar.
       1944) 3.
       Summarizes SA a story "beautifully and simply told."

D141   Review of Steep Ascent. Commonweal, 39 (31 Mar. 1944) 598.
       Examines the link between earth and air.

D142   Hansen, Harry. Survey Graphic, 33 (Apr. 1944) 222.
       Emphasizes the diversity of AML's talents in SA.

D143   Review of Steep Ascent. The Booklist, 40 (1 Apr. 1944) 270.

      Interprets book as a "stream-of-consciousness record of flight."

D144   Review of Steep Ascent. The New Yorker, 20 (1 Apr. 1944) 82.

      Sees book as attention getter.

D145   Review of Steep Ascent. The Bookmark, 5 (1 May 1944) 19.

      Points out creative treatment of cerebral topic.

D146   Review of Steep Ascent. Wisconsin Library Bulletin, 40
      (May 1944) 71.

      Reflects on rhythm of AML's words.

D147   Bregy, Katherine. Catholic World, 159 (May 1944) 184.

      Extols writing talent.

D148   Review of Gift from the Sea. The Book Review Digest, (1955) 556.
      Presents synopsis.

D149   Review of Gift from the Sea. Kirkus Reviews, 23 (1 Feb. 1955) 106.
      Not seen.

D150   Review of Gift from the Sea. Cleveland Open Shelf, (Mar. 1955) 16.
      Not seen.

D151   Blackshear, Orrilla T. Wisconsin Library Bulletin, 51
      (Mar. 1955) 34.

      Describes author of GS growing as a writer.

D152   Willis, K.T. The Library Journal, 80 (1 Mar. 1955) 558.

      Endorses GS for discussion sessions.

D153   Butcher, Fanny. Chicago Sunday Tribune, (13 Mar. 1955) 1.

      Hails GS's importance for both genders.

D154   Review of Gift from the Sea. The Booklist, 51 (15 Mar. 1955) 294.

      Bestows praise on poetic qualities.

D155 Hormel, O.D. Review of <u>Gift from the Sea</u>. <u>Christian Science</u>
      <u>Monitor</u>, 47 (17 Mar. 1955) 7.
      Not seen.

D156 Review of <u>Gift from the Sea</u>. <u>The New York Times</u>, 43 (18 Mar.
      1955) 25.
      Not seen.

D157 Review of <u>Gift from the Sea</u>. <u>The New Yorker</u>, 31 (19 Mar. 1955) 152.
      Values style but not content.

D158 Chase, M.E. <u>The New York Herald Tribune Book Review</u>, (20 Mar. 1955)
      Upholds universal appeal of <u>GS</u>.

D159 Vining, Elizabeth Gray. <u>The New York Times Book Review</u>, 60
      (20 Mar. 1955) 1.
      Regards <u>GS</u> suitable for all readers.

D160 Review of <u>Gift from the Sea</u>. <u>Time Magazine</u>, 65 (21 Mar. 1955) 104.
      Salutes mode of expression.

D161 Jackson, J.H. <u>San Francisco Chronicle</u>, (22 Mar. 1955) 22.
      Praises sensitivity of author of <u>GS</u>.

D162 Brody, M.P. <u>Catholic World</u>, 181 (Apr. 1955) 76.
      Pronounces <u>GS</u> appealingly written.

D163 Weeks, Edward. <u>Atlantic</u>, 195 (Apr. 1955) 76.
      Empathizes with feelings and thoughts expressed in <u>GS</u>.

D164 Hay, Sara Henderson. <u>Saturday Review</u>, 38 (2 Apr. 1955) 22.
      Focuses on "personality" of AML giving <u>GS</u> "real distinction."

D165 Holzhauer, Jean. <u>Commonweal</u>, 62 (8 Apr. 1955) 22.
      Feels <u>GS</u> is a symbol for self-examination.

D166 Dexter, Ethel. Springfield Republican, (10 Apr. 1955) 6.

Review of GS. Not seen.

D167 Review of Gift from the Sea. Newsweek, 45 (11 Apr. 1955) 116-7.

Includes recommendation for male readers.

D168 Review of Gift from the Sea. The Bookmark, 14 (May 1955) 186-7.

Emphasizes "poetic prose."

D169 Review of GS. The Times /London/ Literary Supplement, (28 Oct. 1955) 637.

States book contains some "fruitful ideas."

D170 Lane, Margaret. The New Statesman and Nation, 50 (29 Oct.
1955) 549.

Acclaims GS as "perceptive and profound."

D171 A.M.D. Manchester Guardian, (2 Dec. 1955) 9.

Diminishes GS's importance as belonging to pop psychology genre.

D172 "The Summing Up for '55 Books by the Pound." Newsweek, 46
(26 Dec. 1955) 68-9.

Reports on popularity of GS.

D173 Review of The Unicorn.and Other Poems. The New York Herald Tribune
Book Review, (1956) 572.

Remarks on theme and number of poems in book.

D174 "The Most Successful Women of 1955." Woman's Home Companion,
83 (Jan. 1956) 31.

Praises AML for writing in GS.

D175 Review of The Unicorn and Other Poems. Kirkus Reviews, 24
(1 Aug. 1956) 551.

Believes in the growth of AML's writing.

D176   Review of UOP. The Booklist, 53 (1 Sept. 1956) 11.

Sees pertinence to women's issues.

D177   Richart, Bette. Commonweal, 64 (7 Sept. 1956) 568-570.

Degrades UOP, in sexist attack, as domestic drivel.

D178   Hillyer, Robert. "A Unicorn With Porcelain Hoofs." The New

York Times Book Review, (9 Sept. 1956) 10.

Draws a parallel link to Browning's philosophy.

D179   Holmes, John. The New York Herald Tribune Book Review,

(9 Sept. 1956) 4.

Commends AML on insight manifested in UOP.

D180   MacFall, Russell. Chicago Sunday Tribune, (9 Sept. 1956) 8.

Salutes UOP "destined for popularity."

D181   Bellows, S.B. Christian Science Monitor, (13 Sept. 1956) 11.

Considers UOP terse.

D182   "Better Than Biscuits." Time, 68 (17 Sept. 1956) 106.

Supports UOP for its "sensibility."

D183   Dorn, N.K. Review of UOP. San Francisco Chronicle,

(18 Sept. 1956) 21.

Not seen.

D184   Review of UOP. The Bookmark, 16 (Oct. 1956) 6.

Labels poems "exquisite."

D185   "Anne Morrow Lindbergh-Her Life Story in Pictures." McCall's,

84 (Oct. 1956) 48-53.

D186   McDonald, G.D. The Library Journal, 81 (1 Oct. 1956) 2261.

Predicts popular interest in UOP.

D187   Jacobsen, Josephine. Commonweal, 65 (12 Oct. 1956) 48-49.

       Admits to reading AML's poem.

D188   Dexter, Ethel. Review of UOP. Springfield Republican,

       (14 Oct. 1956) 10.

       Not seen.

D189   Sullivan, A.M. Catholic World, 184 (Nov. 1956) 155.

       Makes reference to "interlinear control" in UOP.

D190   Weeks, Edward. Atlantic, 198 (Nov. 1956) 96.

       Regards UOP effectively concise.

D191   Review of UOP. The New Yorker, 32 (17 Nov. 1956) 243-4.

       Treasures lyrics for their simplicity and sincerity.

D192   Review of UOP. Cleveland Open Shelf, (Dec. 1956) 4.

       Not seen.

D193   Adams, James Donald. Triumph Over Odds. New York: Duell,

       Sloan and Pearce, 1957, p. 435.

       Prefers AML as a "prose stylist," although he finds "charm"

       in UOP.

D194   Wright, Helen and Samuel Rapport. The Great Explorers. New

       York: Harper & Brothers, Publishers, 1957, pp. 594-5.

       Review of Listen! the Wind. Acclaims account peerless.

D195   Ciardi, John. Saturday Review, 40 (12 Jan. 1957) 54-7..

       Details reasons for labeling UOP an "offensively bad book."

D196   Ciardi, John. "The Reviewer's Duty to Damn/A Letter to an

       Avalanche." Saturday Review, 40 (16 Feb. 1957) 24-5, 54-5.

       Defends position taken on UOP on 12 January 1957.

D197   Cousins, Norman. "John Ciardi and the Readers." Saturday
       Review, 40 (16 Feb. 1957) 22-3.
       Defends AML's artistry.

D198   Skardon, J.A. and R. McVay. "Flight from Fame." Coronet, 42
       (July 1957) 30-43.
       Not seen.

D199   Review of Dearly Beloved. Kirkus Reviews, 30 (15 Apr. 1962) 395.
       Not seen.

D200   Stiles, Patricia P. The Library Journal, 87 (1 June 1962) 2157.
       Thinks DB interesting although verbose.

D201   Hogan, William. San Francisco Chronicle, (6 June 1962) 41.
       Confesses DB is not "my kind of book."

D202   Hutchens, John K. Book World, (6 June 1962) 23.
       Review of DB.
       Not seen.

D203   Review of DB. Time, 79 (8 June 1962) 92.
       Disappointed in lack of insight.

D204   Review of DB. The New Yorker, 38 (9 June 1962) 138.
       Questions genre: "less a novel than a collection of little
       talks about love."

D205   Pippett, Aileen. Saturday Review, 45 (9 June 1962) 36.
       Relegates DB to journeyman status.

D206   Butcher, Fanny. Chicago Sunday Tribune Magazine, (10 June 1962) 1
       Observes simple truths give DB its "irresistible appeal."

D207 Peterson, Virgilia. The New York Times Book Review,
      (10 June 1962) 6, 22-3.
      Has problem with genre: DB "not a novel but an essay in disguise."

D208 Rogers, W.G. The New York Herald Tribune Books, 38 (10 June 1962) 8.
      Minimizes worth of DB because of lack of a specific marriage.

D209 Review of DB. Newsweek, 59 (11 June 1962) 101.
      Concludes AML writes with "taste."

D210 Prescott, Orville. The New York Times, 111 (13 June 1962) 39.
      Believes DB has limited reader appeal.

D211 Review of DB. The Booklist, 58 (15 June 1962) 718.
      Finds appeal mainly feminine.

D212 Marsh, Pamela. Christian Science Monitor, (21 June 1962) 7.
      Reduces DB to "interesting experiment."

D213 Swenson, Ruth P. Wisconsin Library Bulletin, 58 (July 1962)
      237-8.
      Recognizes ability to describe emotions common to all humans.

D214 Jackson, Katherine Glauss. Harper's Magazine, (July 1962) 92-3.
      Impressed with imagery in DB.

D215 Weeks, Edward. Atlantic, 210 (July 1962) 108.
      Considers the close in DB a "letdown."

D216 Merritt, E. National Review, 13 (14 Aug. 1962) 110.
      Draws a parallel link between DB and "Mozartian delicacy of strength."

D217 Kiley, Frederick S. Clearing House, 37 (Oct. 1962) 124.
      Finds little of importance in DB.

D218   Ciardi, John.   "The Unicorn: A Close Look at the Unicorn."
       John Ciardi: Dialogue with an Audience. Philadelphia and
       New York: J.B. Lippincott Co., 1963, pp. 74-9
       Takes to task not Mrs. AML, but the quality of her poems.

D219   Ciardi, John.   "The Reviewer's Duty to Damn Letter to an
       Avalanche." John Ciardi: Dialogue with an Audience.
       Philadelphia and New York: J.B. Lippincott Co., 1963, pp. 89-97.
       Upholds prerogative to criticize UOP.

D220   Cousins, Norman. "John Ciardi and the Readers." John Ciardi:
       Dialogue with an Audience. Philadelphia and New York: J.B.
       Lippincott Co., 1963, pp. 84-7.
       Responds to John Ciardi's choice of word "illiterate" by
       calling attention to AML's sensitive use of the English
       language.

D221   Brophy, Brigid. New Statesman, (5 Apr. 1963) 497-8.
       Evinces sarcasm toward DB.

D222   Review of Gift from the Sea. Publishers Weekly, 189
       (10 Jan. 1966) 90-1.
       Acclaims "lucid prose."

D223   Review of Earth Shine. Kirkus Reviews, 37 (15 Aug. 1969) 909.
       Lulled by cadence.

D224   Review of Earth Shine. Publishers Weekly, 196 (8 Sept. 1969) 50.
       Describes AML as "always the poetic observer."

D225 Steen, Signe L. The Library Journal Book Review, 94
      (15 Oct. 1969) 359.
      Places equal value on ES, NO, and GS.

D226 Review of Earth Shine. Time, 94 (24 Oct. 1969) 110.
      Considers AML given to "expostulation."

D227 Cosgrave, M.S. Horn Book Magazine, 45 (Dec. 1969) 698-9.
      Perceives ES "intensely moving."

D228 Collier, Carmen P. Best Sellers, 29 (1 Dec. 1969) 344.
      Assigns ES to "coffee table book" status.

D229 Review of ES. The Booklist, 66 (15 Dec. 1969) 487.
      Finds synthesis of conflicting forces.

D230 Riga, Peter J. The Catholic World, 210 (Jan. 1970) 184.
      Describes ES as overpriced and a restatement of previously
      published material.

D231 Fuller, Edmund. The Wall Street Journal, 175 (18 Feb. 1970) 18.
      Interested in color and halftone photographs in ES.

D232 McCreedy, JoAnn. Catholic Library World, 41 (Apr. 1970) 528.
      Remarks on excellence of total ES.

D233 Story, Elizabeth. The Library Journal, 95 (15 Apr. 1970) 1664.
      Feels ES too simplistic.

D234 Review of ES. Publishers Weekly, 198 (5 Oct. 1970) 65.
      Impressed with "musings."

D235 Review of ES. The Times Literary Supplement, (26 Feb. 1971) 254.
      Prefers second essay for its "poetic style."

D236 Review of Bring Me a Unicorn. Kirkus Reviews, 39 (15 Dec. 1971) 1351.
      Finds it "impossible to cut through the cloy."

D237   A.P.H.   Review of <u>Bring Me a Unicorn</u>. <u>Publishers Weekly</u>, 200
       (20 Dec. 1971) 45.

       Refers to AML's ambition as a writer.

D238   Gambee, Ruth R.   <u>The Library Journal Book Review</u>, 97 (1 Feb.
       1972) 491.

       Feels narrow focus of <u>BMU</u> a powerful means of expression.

D239   Stafford, Jean. <u>Book World</u>, 6 (20 Feb. 1972) 1, 3, 9.

       Decides <u>BMU</u> reaches new heights.

D240   Bevington, Helen. <u>The New York Times Book Review</u>, (27 Feb. 1972)
       3.

       Endorses choice of material in <u>BMU</u>.

D241   Pritchard, Lael. <u>Best Sellers</u>, 31 (1 Mar. 1972) 539.

       Review of <u>BMU</u>. Not seen.

D242   Review of BMU. <u>The Christian Century</u>, 89 (1 Mar. 1972) 259.

       Approves use of photographs.

D243   Millar, Neil. <u>Christian Science Monitor</u>, 64 (2 Mar. 1972) 10.

       Determines every page of <u>BMU</u> worth reading.

D244   Culligan, Glendy. <u>Saturday Review</u>, 55 (4 Mar. 1972) 72, 75.

       Sees in <u>BMU</u> expression of innermost feeling.

D245   Maddocks, Melvin. Review of <u>BMU</u>. <u>Life</u>, 72 (10 Mar. 1972) 24.

       Ridicules lack of discipline.

D246   L.M.   <u>Time</u>, 99 (27 Mar. 1972) 100.

       Reduces <u>BMU</u> to feminine appeal.

D247   Review of <u>BMU</u>. <u>The New Yorker</u>, 48 (1 Apr. 1972) 108.

       Contends feminine readers will feel nostalgia.

D248 Cousins, Margaret. "Love in the Skies." Vogue, 159
      (1 Apr. 1972) 64, 68.
      Applauds BMU for literary renown.

D249 Fuller, Edmund. The Wall Street Journal, 179 (11 Apr. 1972) 22.
      Describes uniqueness of BMU.

D250 Review of BMU. The Booklist, 68 (1 May 1972) 747.
      Sees possibility of future development.

D251 Chamberlain, John. "Old-fashioned girl." National Review,
      24 (12 May 1972) 528.
      Ranks BMU a "love story."

D252 Review of BMU. The Booklist, 68 (15 May 1972) 817.
      Believes BMU is impoverished in thought and style.

D253 Review of BMU. American Libraries, 3 (June 1972) 682.
      Reviews book as study of self.

D254 Cosgrave, Mary Silva. Horn Book Magazine, 48 (June 1972) 293-4.
      Considers style of BMU uninhibited.

D255 Review of BMU. The Times Literary Supplement, 3 (11 Aug.
      1972) 936.
      Points out elements of insight.

D256 Review of Hour of Gold, Hour of Lead. Kirkus Reviews, 41
      (1 Jan. 1973) 43.
      Ranks story a record of history.

D257 Review of HGHL. Publishers Weekly, 203 (1 Jan. 1973) 55.
      Observes subject matter factual.

D258 Gambee, Ruth R. The Library Journal Book Review,
      98 (1 Feb. 1973) 416.
      Submits that tedious style might be inevitable in HGHL.

D259   Stafford, Jean. Book World, 7 (25 Feb. 1973) 1, 6, 7.

Scrutinizes words in HGHL as an exercise bordering on a

"morality play."

D260   Stafford, Jean. McCall's, 100 (Mar. 1973) 80-1, 108, 110-4.

Lauds personal treatment in HGHL.

D261   Kazin, Alfred. The New York Times Book Review, (4 Mar. 1973) 1, 10

Feels one question is not answered in HGHL.

D262   Review of Bring Me a Unicorn. Publishers Weekly, 203

(5 Mar. 1973) 84.

Impressed with narrative style.

D263   Review of HGHL. The Christian Century, 90 (7 Mar. 1973) 297.

Predicts popularity of book.

D264   Millar, Neil. Christian Science Monitor, 65 (7 Mar. 1973) 13.

Suggests information in HGHL is self-revealing.

D265   Fuller, Edmund. The Wall Street Journal, 181 (9 Mar. 1973) 6.

Observes traits of wisdom in HGHL.

D266   Freemantle, Anne. America, 128 (17 Mar. 1973) 246-7.

Comments on HGHL being a "nourishing book."

D267   Janeway, Elizabeth. Saturday Review, 1 (17 Mar. 1973) 76-7.

Cites integrity as pulling power of HGHL.

D268   Pave, Irene. Business Weekly, (24 Mar. 1973) 8, 10.

Reports on emotions expressed by author in HGHL.

D269   Sarton, Mary. Vogue, 161 (Apr. 1973) 63, 95.

Respects ability to relate details in HGHL.

D270   Weeks, Edward. Atlantic Monthly, 231 (Apr. 1973) 124-5.

Points candid quality expressed in HGHL.

D271 Hill, Irene. Best Sellers, 33 (1 Apr. 1973) 15.

Upholds points in HGHL worthy of contemplation.

D272 Review of HGHL. The New Yorker, 49 (14 Apr. 1973) 156.

Comments on strength of character.

D273 Hentoff, Margot. The New York Times Review of Books, 20

(19 Apr. 1973) 3.

Review of HGHL. Not seen.

D274 Russ, Lavinia. Review of HGHL. Retirement Living, 13

(May 1973) 17-8,60. .

Inspires readers in the face of adversity.

D275 Review of HGHL. America, 128 (5 May 1973) 418.

Values contrast between hope and tragedy.

D276 Review of BMU. Book World, 7 (6 May 1973) 14.

Sees Bring Me a Unicorn having reader appeal.

D277 Review of HGHL. The Booklist, 69 (15 May 1973) 884.

Enjoys "her sense of humor."

D278 Review of HGHL. The Library Journal Index, 89 (24 May 1973) 694.

Gives synopsis of book.

D279 Tennant, Emma. The Listener London Weekly, 89 (24 May 1973) 694-5.

Suggests that Truman Capote should have written about this

tragedy in HGHL.

D280 Review of HGHL. The Progressive, 37 (June 1973) 58.

Hails with satisfaction.

D281 Cosgrave, Mary Silva. Horn Book Magazine, 49 (June 1973) 297.

Marks HGHL a profound book.

D282   Lund, Sister Candida. The Critic, 31 (May/June 1973) 67-9..
       Defines HGHL lettre de cachet.

D283   Review of HGHL. The New York Times Book Review, (10 June 1973) 36
       Renders book graphic.

D284   Leonard, John. The New York Times Book Review, (10 June 1973) 4.
       Indicates HGHL has "1930's" historical value.

D285   Review of HGHL. The Times Literary Supplement (29 June 1973) 735.
       Portrays book as dolorific.

D286   Review of HGHL. Choice, 10 (Sept. 1973) 980.
       Takes cognizance of material reminders.

D287   Review of HGHL. The New York Times Book Review, (2 Dec. 1973) 70.
       Acknowledges strong emotions of book.

D288   Review of HGHL. The Book Review Digest, (1974) 723.
       Writes synopsis.

D289   Squire, C.B. "Heroes of Conservation." Fleet Press, (1974) 72-9.
       Not seen.

D290   Zelenko, Barbara. The Library Journal Book Review, (1974) 111.
       Impressed with integrity of AML expressed in Locked Rooms and
       Open Doors.

D291   Eisenhower, Julie Nixon. The Saturday Evening Post, 246
       (Jan./Feb. 1974) 22.
       Calls attention to AML's abstract qualities.

D292   Review of LROD. Kirkus Reviews, 42 (1 Jan. 1974) 41.
       Remarks that readers will be attracted because of feminine style.

D293   Review of LROD. Publishers Weekly, 205 (14 Jan. 1974) 91.
       Predicts commercial benefits.

D294 Stafford, Jean. "Anne Lindbergh: A Puzzlement." <u>Vogue</u>, 163
      (Mar. 1974) 38.
      Characterizes report of self "superficial."

D295 Howard, Jane. "Out of the Blue." <u>Book World</u>, (10 Mar. 1974) 1.
      Ranks <u>LROd</u> as "valuable document."

D296 Kazin, Alfred. <u>The New York Times Book Review</u>, (10 Mar. 1974) 33.
      Considers <u>HGHL</u> written by a person capable of expressing
      emotions.

D297 Baker, A.T. "So Well Remembered." <u>Time</u>, 103 (11 Mar. 1974) 11.
      Says <u>HGHL</u> manifests precision of AML's writing.

D298 Fuller, Edmund. <u>The Wall Street Journal</u>, 183 (15 Mar. 1974) 6.
      Calls <u>HGHL</u> a "rare American chronicle."

D299 Stimpson, Catharine R. <u>The New York Times Book Review</u>, 7
      (24 Mar. 1974) 28, 30.
      Explains that although many of the entries in <u>LROD</u> are written
      without restraint, there are parts that need to be expatiated.

D300 Review of <u>LROD</u>. <u>The New Yorker</u>, 50 (25 Mar. 1974) 143-4.
      Decides theme timeless.

D301 Whitman, Alden. "To Watch a Person Uncurl." <u>The New York
      Times</u>, 123 (30 Mar. 1974) 29.
      States that moments in <u>LROD</u> seem "too storybook."

D302 Millar, Neil. <u>Christian Science Monitor</u>, 66 (3 Apr. 1974) 5.
      Ascertains that <u>LROD</u> draws a picture of pathos.

D303 Hill, Irene R. <u>Best Sellers</u>, 34 (15 Apr. 1974) 34.
      Finds <u>LROD</u> unattractive because of its repetiveness.

D304 Freemantle, Anne. America, 130 (20 Apr. 1974) 311.

Likens reading LROD to "hearing Bach."

D305 Zelenko, Barbara. The Library Journal, 99 (1 May 1974) 1294.

Calls attention to integrity manifested by AML in writing LROD.

D306 Review of LROD. America, 130 (4 May 1974) 348.

Points out AML's sensitivity.

D307 Review of LROD. The Booklist, 70 (15 May 1974) 1028.

Feels readers of AML's earlier books will not be disappointed.

D308 Review of LROD. The Progressive, 38 (June 1974) 60.

Distinguishes book as a fluent, convincing "exploration" of
AML's "selfhood."

D309 Cosgrave, Mary Silva. Horn Book Magazine, 50 (June 1974) 304-5
Recognizes quality of introspection in LROD.

D310 Weeks, Edward. Atlantic Monthly, 233 (June 1974) 111-2.
Pronounces AML's LROD presents her "better in action than in
repining."

D311 Coyne, Patricia S. "The Urge to Disengage." National Review,
26 (21 June 1974) 712-3.

Suggests LROD is not a "feminist tract."

D312 Review of LROD. Choice, 11 (July 1974) 743.

Presents book "not recommended for higher academe."

D313 Genett, Ann. "Contributions of Women: Aviation." Dillon Press,
(1975) 22-37.

Not seen.

D314 "Gift from the Sea." McCall's, 102 (Aug. 1975) 75-6, 107-112.

Reports on book's ultimate response.

D315   Review of <u>The Flower and the Nettle</u>. <u>Kirkus Reviews</u>, 43
       (15 Dec. 1975) 1416.

       Decides analytic treatment unclear.

D316   Review of <u>FN</u>. <u>The Book Review Digest</u>, (1976) 717.

       Gives synopsis.

D317   Zelenko, Barbara. <u>The Library Book Review</u>, (1976) 115.

       Suggests author of <u>FN</u> should adhere to more personal approach.

D318   Review of <u>FN</u>. <u>Publishers Weekly</u>, 209 (5 Jan. 1976) 61.

       Notices author's gift for communicating emotion.

D319   Review of <u>FN</u>. <u>The Booklist</u>, 72 (15 Jan. 1976) 663.

       Commends AML for clearness of insight.

D320   Review of <u>FN</u>. <u>The Booklist</u>, 72 (15 Jan. 1976) 680.

       Urges readers of AML's other diaries to "read this one."

D321   Hahn, Emily. <u>The New York Times Book Review</u>, 441 (22 Feb.
       1976) 3, 28.

       Questions method of presentation and movement of <u>FN</u>, "this ...
       interesting story."

D322   Levine, Joe Ann. <u>Christian Science Monitor</u>, 68 (23 Feb.
       1976) 22.

       Impressed with AML's gift for making ordinary, special in <u>FN</u>.

D323   Fuller, Edmund. Review of <u>FN</u>. <u>The Wall Street Journal</u>, 187
       (26 Feb. 1976) 16.

       Recognizes author's perspicuity.

D324   Freemantle, Anne. <u>America</u>, 134 (28 Feb. 1976) 162.

       Believes AML holds firmly to her stand on issues in <u>FN</u>.

D325   Zelenko, Barbara. The Library Journal, 101 (15 Mar. 1976) 806.

       Hurls criticism at domestic detail in FN.

D326   Sheppard, R.Z. Time, 107 (29 Mar. 1976) 72, 74.

       Repeats AML's quotation of Reike's "tart definition of fame."

D327   Review of FN. The Progressive, 40 (May 1976) 45.

       Pleased with richness of reflection; disappointed, however,

       with cumbersome details.

D328   Spindle, Donna J. Best Sellers, 36 (May 1976) 47.

       Perceives style "smooth and personal," in FN.

D329   Whitman, Alden. Ladies Home Journal, 93 (May 1976) 68, 70,

       178, 180, 186.

       Declares AML has "mastered the writer's exacting craft."

D330   Chamberlain, John. National Review, 28 (14 May 1976) 518.

       Respects AML's superiority as a commentator in FN.

D331   Review of FN. Choice, 13 (June 1976) 583.

       Recommends for universal appeal.

D332   McCarthy, Abigail. Ms, 4 (June 1976) 46-7.

       Questions relevance of FN but values thoughts on women.

D333   Review of FN. The Observer, 1 (8 Aug. 1976) 21.

       Not seen.

D334   Review of FN. Saturday Evening Post, 248 (Oct. 1976) 77.

       Recommends book.

D335   Mosley, Diana. Books and Bookmen, 22 (Dec. 1976) 16-8.

       Finds AML verbose and FM unimportant.

D336   Clark, Lindley H., Jr.   The Wall Street Journal, 188
       (8 Dec. 1976) 24.
       Observes interest in FN has not diminished.

D337   Lipscomb, Elizabeth Johnston.   "The Flower and the Nettle."
       Magill's Literary Annual 1977. Englewood Cliffs, New Jersey:
       Salem Press, 1977, pp. 294-7.
       Discusses historical value of FN.

D338   Magill, Frank Northern, ed.   "Gift from the Sea." Survey of
       Contemporary Literature. Englewood Cliffs, New Jersey:
       Salem Press, 1977, pp. 2937-9.
       Calls work "Belles-letters," and praises writing for poetic
       qualities.

D339   Nelson, Alix.   The New York Times Book Review, 441
       (3 Apr. 1977) 22.
       Pleased with AML's "androgynous vision of the future" in
       Gift from the Sea.

D340   Whitman, Alden.   "Anne Morrow Lindbergh Reminisces About Life
       With Lindy."   The New York Times Magazine, (8 May 1977)
       16-8, 22, 26, 28.

D341   Thrush, Robin.   "A Hero's Wife Remembers."   Good Housekeeping,
       184 (June 1977) 74, 76, 78, 80, 82.
       Considers Gift from the Sea attuned to the needs and
       "yearnings of women."

INDEX